WESTMINSTER ABBEY

The interior, looking east from the choir screen.

The New Bell's Cathedral Guides

WESTMINSTER ABBEY

CHRISTOPHER WILSON
PAMELA TUDOR-CRAIG
JOHN PHYSICK
RICHARD GEM

PHOTOGRAPHY BY MALCOLM CROWTHERS

Bell & Hyman

Acknowledgements

The authors, photographer and publishers wish to thank the following organizations and individuals for their help: Dean and Chapter of Westminster Abbey, and all the Abbey staff; Martin and Birth Biddle, Tony Cutler, David Dovey, English Heritage, J. Peter Foster, Professor Philip Grierson, Albert and Jaqueline Heckford, Sandy Heslop, Richard Hodges, Keith Johnson Photographic Ltd, Maureen Jupp, Deborah Kahn, David Mason, Enid Nixon, Kenneth Oakley, Black Rod's office in the Palace of Westminster, Robert Taylor, Alan Vince, George Wagstaff and Jeffrey West. All the photographs in the book were taken by Malcolm Crowthers, with the exception of the following: The Society of Antiquaries 21, 104; Terry Ball 16 above; with special authorization of the town of Bayeux 14; The British Architectural Library, RIBA, London 46; Conway Library, The Courtauld Institute of Art with permission from the Syndics of Cambridge University Library 118; Royal Commission on the Historical Monuments of England 71; by Courtesy of the Dean and Chapter of Westminster 44 right, 45 left. Artwork by Gareth Jones.

First published 1986 by
Bell & Hyman Limited
Denmark House
37-39 Queen Elizabeth Street
London SE1 2QB

© Christopher Wilson
Pamela Tudor-Craig
John Physick
Richard Gem 1986

Photographs © Malcolm Crowthers

Designed by Colin Lewis
Typeset by Typecast Photosetting & Printing Ltd., East Peckham, Kent
Printed in Great Britain at the University Press, Cambridge

ISBN 7135 2612 2 (cased)

7135 26130 (limp)

British Library Cataloguing in Publication Data

Westminster Abbey — (The new Bell's cathedral guides)
1. Westminster Abbey — Guide-books 2. London
(England) — Churches
I. Wilson, Christopher, 1948
914.21'32 DA687.W5

CONTENTS

Chapter One

THE ORIGINS OF THE ABBEY

THE FOUNDATION OF WESTMINSTER

Thorney Island and its Roman Remains

WESTMINSTER LIES ON what was once a small gravel island, Thorney Island, marked off from the rest of the Thames shoreline by two streams of the River Tyburn. It was probably here that the earliest crossing of the Thames in the region was located — perhaps already in the pre-Roman period. When, however, the Romans built their bridge and established their city of *Londinium* it was some two miles further down the river.

Evidence was discovered in the nineteenth century which has been thought to show that Thorney Island was the site of substantial Roman buildings, but no plan was made of these and it may be that they were later structures which re-used Roman building materials. Also discovered at Westminster have been two Roman funerary monuments, one of which was a probably third-century sarcophagus (subsequently re-used) inscribed:

> MEMORIAE. VALER. AMAN
> DINI. VALERI. SVPERVEN
> TOR. ET. MARCELLVS. PATRI. FECER.

(In memory of Valerius Amandinus, the Valerii, Superventor and Marcellus, made this for their father).

From Roman to Anglo-Saxon London

Current archaeological evidence suggests that the once flourishing Roman City was already in decline from the late third and early fourth centuries onwards, well before it ceased to be an important administrative centre of Roman Britain. Thus it may have been as much economic failure as armed aggression that led to the eventual

The third century sarcophagus of Valerius Amandinus: probable evidence of Westminster's Roman antecedents. The lid belongs to a medieval re-use. In the foreground are the medieval tiles of the Pyx chamber floor.

depopulation of the walled City, while in the surrounding countryside the remaining Romano-British population eventually (but at an uncertain date) passed under the control of pagan Anglo-Saxon settlers from North Germany and Denmark.

By the early seventh century the 'Middle Saxons' north of the Thames (Middlesex) had been absorbed into the kingdom of the East Saxons, while their kinsmen south of the river (Surrey, the South District) retained a degree more of independence: both alike, however, were subject to the political control of more powerful neighbours. Thus it was Æthelberht, the first Christian king of Kent, who in 604 established a bishopric for the East and Middle Saxons and installed Mellitus, an Italian monk who had come to Kent to assist Archbishop Augustine of Canterbury, in London as their bishop. According to later tradition this was the time at which Westminster was founded, but the reliability of this can only be assessed by considering further the historical background.

When King Æthelberht died in 616 (and his vassal King Saeberht of the East Saxons at about the same time) there was a pagan reaction: Mellitus was expelled from his diocese and was never permitted to return by the inhabitants of London. New missionaries were sent into the area in the 650s, but it was not until the 660s that there seems to have been a bishopric in London again — by which time control over the region was passing from the kings of Kent to those of the powerful midland kingdom of Mercia.

The enduring foundations of the Christian church in London were laid towards the end of the seventh century by Earconwald, who was appointed bishop *c.* 675, having previously founded important monasteries in the vicinity of London at Barking and Chertsey. In connection with the latter the bishop obtained a royal grant of land which included an area 'near the port of London, where ships come to land', and this is the earliest unambiguous documentary reference to the revival of London as a trading place in the Anglo-Saxon period — although its developing economic status as early as the 640s may be suggested by the minting there of gold coins. However, what is of capital importance for understanding Westminster is that the new port was not located where the Roman and later medieval City of London stood: rather it seems to have occupied the area between the City and Westminster Abbey, and is commemorated in street names such as Aldwych ('the old town') and the Strand ('the shore,' where the boats drew up).

By around 730 London was known to Bede as a 'trading centre for many nations who come to it by land and sea' and control of this trade must have seemed increasingly desirable to the kings of land-locked Mercia. Thus, perhaps under King Æthelbald (716-757) who was certainly able to take a toll on ships coming into the port, London was fully incorporated into Mercia. In some measure the trade through London may have contributed to sustaining an economy which allowed the rise of Mercia under Æthelbald and his great successor, Offa (757-796), to a predominant political position among the kingdoms of England, and to an international status that placed it on a footing with the powerful Carolingian Franks. By 811 London's importance is suggested by a contemporary description of it as 'the famous place and royal city, London town'.

The Foundation of the West Minster

Westminster (that is, the West Minster in distinction from the East Minster of St Paul's — 'minster' being the Anglo-Saxon word deriving from the Latin *monasterium*, a monastery) was set in a crucial geographical position in relation to the London of the seventh and eighth centuries. What is more, the Minster can be seen later as holding in its possession most of the area of land occupied by the settlement and port. The question this raises is whether Westminster was the original mother church of London, losing its role to the cathedral church of the diocese only when the City was repopulated in the late ninth century.

The earliest account of the foundation that has come down to us is that written sometime between 1076 and 1085 by the Westminster monk Sulcard. According to this King Æthelberht, after founding St Paul's Cathedral in 604, wished to found also a church in honour of St Peter. At this juncture a citizen of London and his wife asked if they might build this church, and subsequently they duly constructed it on Thorney Island. Bishop Mellitus was asked to dedicate the completed building, but was forestalled by St Peter himself who performed the ceremony in the course of a nocturnal visitation from heaven.

From this it seems that Sulcard was ignorant of the name of the founder. He did not attribute the foundation directly to AEethelberht or Mellitus, but adduced an anonymous citizen (whom only later tradition converted into King Sæberht). Sulcard set his narrative in the early seventh century presumably because this was the earliest date he could plausibly claim: but he was careful not to force the details so far that they could be challenged by reference to Bede.

If the earliest historical sources are thus all but silent on the circumstances of the foundation, we today can do little more than speculate until such time as archaeology provides more data: the present account provides, therefore, only a hypothesis to be tested by future work. At an uncertain date, but at one likely to be related to the growth of the Anglo-Saxon settlement and port of London, a church was founded on Thorney Island, possibly attracted there by the ruins of Roman buildings which offered a good source of materials. This could not have been before the time of Bishop Mellitus, but it could have been actually at this early date if Mellitus had wished to found a suburban monastery on the pattern of Canterbury: the silence of Bede, however, may be against this. The more likely possibility is that the foundation took place sometime after the middle of the seventh century as an initiative of the Mercian or East Saxon kings; or of the bishops of London; or (following Sulcard) of a leading member of the local community in London, the influence of which is hinted at by Bede.

Confirmation that Westminster was in existence anyway by the late eighth century may be provided by a charter which was claimed to have been granted by King Offa. This document is now lost but is described in another, tenth-century, charter: 'an ancient charter of freedom which King Offa once granted to the monastery at that time when, on the advice of Archbishop Wulfred, he ordered charters to be written for the churches through all the regions of the English restoring their privileges'. The only difficulty is that Archbishop Wulfred (805-832) cannot have been named in a charter of Offa, who died in 796: on the other hand, Wulfred could have confirmed a charter earlier granted by Offa. Wulfred is known to have been deeply concerned with restoring Church control over the monasteries of England, many of which had fallen under secular domination, and to this end he held an important reforming Synod at Chelsea in 816. Offa on the other hand believed firmly in royal control of the Church: but he was nonetheless a benefactor and founder of monasteries and minsters and could certainly have granted an important charter to Westminster.

In the tenth century it was claimed that Offa's grant to Westminster comprised an area of land stretching from the Tyburn eastward to the Fleet, and from the Thames northward to Oxford Street. It included thus the principal area of Anglo-Saxon London and this raises the question of whether the grant was a confirmation of a previous state of affairs or a totally new departure. If it was a confirmation (as may seem more likely), then we could see the Minster and settlement as having grown up alongside one another in the seventh and eighth centuries. If it was a new grant, however, then it would suggest an exceptionally important policy decision by Offa and would imply a new status for the Minster — if not its actual foundation. However, in view of the uncertainty of the evidence we should be very cautious about accepting the claimed boundaries of Offa's grant as hard historical fact.

The period of Offa and later Wulfred coincided with a significant moment in European culture, when the new Carolingian monarchy of the Frankish kingdom was pioneering a great revival which touched especially upon religious and artistic life. It may well be, therefore, that Westminster in the late eighth and early ninth centuries was caught up in an English expression of this revival. And, if Archbishop Wulfred was involved then it would be difficult to deny the likelihood of some influence from the Continental reforms of Bishop Chrodegang of Metz and Abbot Benedict of Aniane who were seeking to establish a more rigorous discipline in the lives of clergy and monks.

The Viking Period and the New City

Whatever the precise character of Westminster in the early ninth century, any church lying substantially undefended beside the Thames must have presented an easy target for the Danish Viking raiders and armies who shortly started to descend upon England. In 842 and 851 there were attacks upon London; then in the early 870s a concerted campaign effectively destroyed the Mercian kingdom and London came under Viking control. The English counter-attack was eventually led by King Alfred the Great, who retook London in 886 and established there a *burh* or defended borough. This event marked the definitive refoundation of London as an urban community within the defences of the old Roman walled city — which thereafter was to develop as London proper, while the area to the west of it became a suburb. This fundamentally changed the relationship of Westminster to London, and it was St Paul's which thereafter became the great civic church.

In the course of time Westminster was to acquire another role, but in the aftermath of the Vikings its future must have seemed bleak. Its buildings had been damaged and only partially repaired, while at the same time it had lost control of the great London estate granted for its endowment by Offa.

St Dunstan and the Benedictine Abbey

The middle years of the tenth century on the Continent had witnessed in various places a movement towards a reform of monastic life to bring it more into line with the guiding principles of the two great monks Benedict of Nursia (c. 480-550) and Benedict of Aniane (c. 750-821). The ideas of the reformers came to England, especially through the influence of St Dunstan of Glastonbury who, on returning to England in 957 from a period studying in the famous monasteries of Ghent, was appointed Bishop of London by King Edgar. Installed in his see, Dunstan determined to secure the refoundation of Westminster as a Benedictine abbey.

Two steps were essential to open the way for the refoundation. The first was the appointment as abbot of Westminster of someone sympathetic to Dunstan's aims: Wulfsige, a native of London who had been brought up at Westminster and had later made his monastic profession to Dunstan. The second step was for Dunstan to buy back from the king the estate given by Offa and to use this, together with other estates which he had purchased over several years, to create an endowment for the Abbey. Edgar restored the former estate with a charter (preserved among the Abbey muniments in an early copy) which stated that this grant of Westminster to Dunstan was to be used for 'restoring the destroyed *pastoforia* of the church and for setting up the institutions of a monastery, so that henceforward the laws of monastic discipline according to the Rule may be observed there among those leading the regular life'. This was the moment at which Westminster became truly a Benedictine abbey.

The establishment of the Benedictine rule required the provision of suitable domestic buildings in which the monks could lead the communal life and these were duly built by Wulfsige. This could be seen as the work of restoring destroyed buildings referred to in Edgar's charter, but the word *pastoforia* would more naturally apply to side chambers of the church itself, and it may be that work was carried

A tenth- or early eleventh-century copy of King Edgar's (957-975) charter granting Westminster to Bishop Dunstan to found the Benedictine Abbey. The text also refers to King Offa's (757-796) grant and to Archbishop Wulfred (805-832).

out on the latter to restore and adapt it for its new use. However, the church and its attached buildings have never been investigated archaeologically and nothing is known of their actual appearance (though the supposed Roman remains beneath the nave may in fact have been part of the Anglo-Saxon complex).

Little is known of the subsequent history of the new Abbey, but one event may be significant as a prelude to the later role of the church. In 1040 when King Harold I died his body was brought to Westminster for burial — only to be disinterred and thrown into the Thames by his successor (and later recovered again and taken to St Clement Danes). This was the first royal burial in the Abbey and suggests that already before the time of King Edward royal interest in Westminster may have been developing.

KING EDWARD AND THE REBUILDING OF THE ABBEY

Westminster under King Edward

In 1042 there came to the throne of England the last king of the ancient West Saxon dynasty, Edward, the surviving son of AEthelred the Unready. From his early teens, while England was under the rule of Danish kings, Edward had been brought up in exile in his mother's native Normandy, and there he had become imbued with the burgeoning culture of the Normans and of the surrounding areas of France. Two facets of that culture were to be especially important for the future of Westminster: an exciting new style of Romanesque architecture and a reformed monastic and intellectual life.

When Edward returned to England, in his late thirties, its cultural life must have seemed rather conservative compared with the Continent and this no doubt was the psychological factor that led him to plan a great project which would embody the new ideas and proclaim their arrival on this side of the Channel — a project for the total rebuilding of Westminster Abbey. On a more explicit level, however, as Edward's biography (*The Life of King Edward*, written 1065-67) informs us, he decided on the rebuilding because of his devotion to St Peter (the patron saint of Westminster); because of the prominent situation of the place near London and the Thames; and because he planned to be buried there.

Edward's interest in Westminster was probably manifested first in the decade following his accession, and began with his issuing a series of royal writs to confirm and increase the endowments of the Abbey. He also appointed a new abbot, Eadwine, who must have been a man sympathetic to his aims. The most important part of the scheme, however, was the plan for the complete rebuilding of the church — in which he was perhaps encouraged by Bishop Robert of London (1044-1051), who was a great patron of the arts and a famous builder in his native Normandy.

The foundations of the new church were laid out some distance to the east of the old buildings (the latter being presumably somewhere in the region of the west end of the present nave) and were planned so that the east end of the new building — which was most needed for the liturgy — could be completed and brought into use before it was necessary to demolish the old church. The section of the church thus begun and brought to completion in 1065 is described by the *Life of King Edward*. It started with the sanctuary for the high altar, and here the biographer comments on the high quality of the stonework and the many arches — perhaps including a high vault. Further west came the crossing where the choir was situated, with a tower rising above. The flanking transept arms had apsidal chapels, arranged in two storeys the upper of which were reached by galleries. Spiral stairs led to the upper levels, and the transepts had open wooden roofs, covered externally with lead. West of the crossing the first few bays of the nave were begun, and the

Scene from the Bayeux Tapestry of Edward the Confessor's funeral in 1066 at the new Abbey still under construction.

choir probably stretched into these — while the remainder of the nave, being largely a processional space, was not so urgent.

The new building was solemnly dedicated on 28 December 1065, but King Edward was too ill to attend and died a few days later. The funeral procession from Westminster Palace to the place of burial before the high altar of the Abbey is shown in the Bayeux Tapestry, where the church is represented schematically (still without its western towers).

The Norman Conquest

Edward died with no direct heir, leaving a disputed succession between his brother-in-law, Earl Harold, and his cousin, Duke William of Normandy, thus setting in train the events that were to lead to the battle of Hastings and the Norman Conquest of England in 1066. The Conquest could have brought an untimely end to the great project at Westminster: but in fact it did not, no doubt because William saw the valuable role the Abbey could play in propaganda making him out as Edward's rightful successor. Thus William was crowned and anointed as King of England in Westminster Abbey on Christmas Day 1066 — initiating the tradition that made coronation at Westminster a seal of legitimate monarchy in this land.

For probably similar reasons King William pressed ahead with the completion of the new Abbey buildings. Thus in an account written *c.* 1080 the demolition of the old buildings to make way for the termination of the nave is spoken of as a past event, and a completion in the 1070s therefore seems likely. However, the nave was not the only

14

problem requiring attention, for as soon as the monks moved into the new church in 1065 they must have felt the need for new domestic buildings in closer proximity than their old quarters. The new domestic buildings, therefore, are likely to have been put in hand at the same time as the western part of the nave — though their completion may have taken longer. There is evidence that an elaborate cloister was erected between 1087 and 1100, and this may have marked the final stage of the project.

Under William the Conqueror the cross-Channel contacts of the Abbey were strengthened by the appointment of Norman abbots: Geoffrey, formerly abbot of Jumièges; Vitalis, formerly abbot of Bernay; Gilbert Crispin, formerly a monk of Bec. Gilbert especially was a distinguished representative of the tradition of new learning stemming from Bec, whose best known representatives were Lanfranc and Anselm, successively archbishops of Canterbury. As abbot, Gilbert introduced to Westminster the reformed monastic observance compiled by Lanfranc, and this was to form the basis of the religious life at the Abbey through the remainder of the Middle Ages.

The Eleventh-Century Buildings

Of the Early Romanesque buildings of the Abbey only fragments remain for the visitor to see today: but these fragments should by no means be overlooked, on account of their exceptional historical importance. The church itself was entirely demolished in the thirteenth and fourteenth centuries to make way for the present Gothic structure; but enough has been excavated to allow, in conjunction with the documentary descriptions, a reconstruction of its appearance. What is immediately apparent is the enormous length of the church (98.2m or 322ft) which placed it among the largest buildings in Europe in its day. The details of the design, however, insofar as they are known, indicate a specifically close relationship with Normandy and, in the case of the nave, especially with the abbey of Jumièges. It is not difficult to believe, therefore, that Bishop Robert, who before and after his period of office in England was responsible for the rebuilding of Jumièges, helped King Edward to obtain the best masons from Normandy. One of these masons was perhaps Teinfrith the churchwright, whose name indicates his Continental origin. However, other masons had English names: Leofsi Dudde's son, from London, and Godwine Greatsyd. Possibly English masons were quickly trained up by Norman masters to positions of responsibility in the work — and it is worth noting that local resources were exploited for the building materials, with most of the stone coming from a

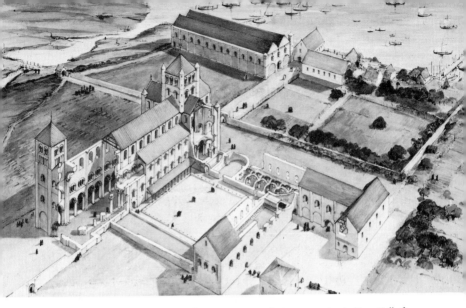

Westminster in the late eleventh century: a watercolour reconstruction by Terry Ball after research by Richard Gem. Beyond the Abbey is to be seen the royal palace.

The barrel vaulted passageway between the Dark Cloister and the Little Cloister, c. 1065-1075.

quarry which must have been opened up near Reigate in Surrey.

It is in the buildings around the cloister, to the south of the nave, that the visitor today can see the most substantial remains of the eleventh-century buildings. The earliest are the structures on the east side, to the south of the chapter house, which probably date to the late 1060s and early 1070s. There is a basement with seven bays of groin vaulting carried on circular columns (today the Abbey museum and the Pyx chamber), then two barrel-vaulted bays (one forming the passage through to the Little Cloister). At first-floor level these vaults carried the monks' dormitory (now used by Westminster School), from which one well-preserved capital survives — perhaps illustrating the type used also in the church.

At the south end of the dormitory was the reredorter or lavatory block, which is now partly demolished but the east wall of which (in the Little Cloister) shows a remarkable use of glazed red tiles to decorate the wall surface. Similar tiles (not accessible to the public) were used on the west wall of the refectory, which ran along the south side of the cloister. Other details of this now largely demolished refectory indicate that it was built later than the dormitory: so the late 1070s or '80s seem likely. To this phase also belongs the partly barrel-vaulted Dark Cloister forming a passageway from the main cloister and running south between the dormitory and refectory ranges (access to the museum is gained from here).

A remarkable capital found in 1807 and subsequently sold and lost appears to have come from the eleventh-century cloister. It bore an inscription referring to the construction of the cloister and other work in the time of Abbot Gilbert Crispin and King William II and this dates it to between 1087 and 1100. The capital depicted the King and the Abbot holding a charter and also the Abbot reading from a liturgical book. Other capitals from the same series survive and are of figurative and foliage types. The finest of the former depicts the *Judgement of Solomon*.

Within the south walk of the cloister took place the burial of all the abbots from Vitalis, *c.* 1085, to William du Hommet, in 1222, and three of these with effigies survive. The earliest (the central one) is that of Gilbert Crispin (1117 or '18) and it formerly bore an inscription that may be translated: 'Here, Gilbert, you lie, an eminent father, born noble and in old age still chaste, a light on the way and a guide to your children. You were meek, just, prudent, steadfast, restrained, wise in learned matters and no less in humble ones. Distinguished thus, yet through death, on the sixth day of December, you give back to heaven your breath and to the earth your bones.'

Capitals probably from the cloister, c. 1087-1100. Three sides of a lost capital showing King William Rufus and Abbot Gilbert Crispin (from an illustration of 1836).

A capital showing a series of scenes from the Judgement of Solomon.

THE CULT OF ST EDWARD THE CONFESSOR

The Making of a Saint

The historical King Edward is a difficult man to appraise through the surviving biographical accounts, but there is enough evidence to suggest that he was a more vigorous and determined monarch than later legend allowed. The subsequent transformation of his image was probably inspired largely by his childlessness which, whatever its real cause, was taken as a sign of abstinence from marital relations with his wife (at that time thought to be a virtue in clerical circles). But also Edward was held to have performed certain miracles of healing sick people — a power which medieval kings generally were believed to receive through their consecration.

Following Edward's death further miracles of healing

Sculptured fragments from the Abbey buildings of the mid- and late twelfth century.

occurred at his tomb and in 1102 the latter was opened to examine his body: it was found incorrupt and this was taken as confirmatory evidence of his chastity. However, it was not until well into the twelfth century that a serious campaign was mounted for Edward's canonization, and this was largely the work of one man, Osbert de Clare, a monk and later prior to Westminster, who had himself received a cure through Edward's intercession. Osbert completed a new biography of Edward in 1138 and secured the support of King Stephen and other influential people to petition the pope for Edward's canonization: but the pope deferred any decision in the matter. There things rested for twenty years until Osbert was able to interest a new abbot, Laurence, in setting up an enquiry into Edward's claimed sanctity. The result was a new petition to Rome, backed by King Henry II, which this time issued in a bull of canonization dated 7 February 1161.

Preparations were then made for a solemn translation of Edward's relics and on 13 October 1163, in the presence of the King, Archbishop Thomas Becket raised Edward's body from the tomb before the high altar and placed it aloft in a shrine of gold and silver which had been presented by William I but which Henry II had had remodelled for the occasion. In this moment St Edward the Confessor attained a pre-eminent position as patron saint of the English monarchy and as a symbol of the final recon-

Tomb effigy of Abbot Gilbert Crispin, d. 1117-18.

ciliation of the Norman and English races a century after the
Conquest.

The Twelfth-Century Buildings

During the years when the cult of St Edward was being promoted
architectural and artistic fashions were changing fast in England and it
is difficult to believe that the eleventh-century buildings of the Abbey
underwent no alterations or updating, but clear evidence for this is

Changing images of Edward the Confessor. LEFT: The king enthroned, on his great seal, c. 1050. RIGHT: The patron saint, on the Abbey seal, c. 1200.

forthcoming in only a few instances. The most important of these was the building of a new infirmary chapel of St Katherine (the ruins of which lie to the east of the Little Cloister), which has been attributed to Abbot Laurence c. 1160. But there is also a documentary record that Henry II gave money for repairs to the monks' refectory south of the main cloister. Possibly related to these works around the two cloisters are a number of surviving sculptured capitals which, with other sculptural fragments (some of them of beautiful quality), date from around the middle and second half of the twelfth century.

Perhaps more important than any work to the domestic buildings, however, were possible alterations to the church itself during the twelfth century. In the first place, archaeological investigation in the nave has shown that the original design of the piers was modified in such a way as to suggest the addition of a new vault over the nave and aisles: but the date of this is unknown. Secondly, at the east end of the church it seems likely (but not conclusive) that the eleventh-century building had a solid apse, whereas by the time that the new thirteenth-century Lady Chapel was begun it was so placed as to require an ambulatory passing round the apse to give access to it. Possibly, therefore, the apse had been modified during the twelfth century, and an occasion for this could have been provided by the enshrinement of St Edward in 1163. Whatever the precise facts may be, we can at least be sure that by the end of the twelfth century the Abbey was filled with art treasures in sculpture, painting and stained glass that provided a resplendent setting for the shrine and complemented the now old-fashioned sobriety of the largely eleventh-century architecture.

Chapter Two

THE GOTHIC ABBEY CHURCH
THE PATRONAGE OF HENRY III

T HE FIRST INDICATION that the Romanesque church was becoming inadequate for the needs of the community it served was the start of work in 1220 on a large Lady Chapel to the east of the main apse. This building was demolished to make way for the present Lady Chapel (Henry VII's Chapel) in 1502-3, and almost all that is known about it is that its west end stood some 10m (30ft) from the eleventh-century apse. The interval was probably occupied in part by an ambulatory, since the building accounts mention a chapel of St Adrian and St Michael above the main chapel, an arrangement difficult to understand unless there were ambulatories at aisle and gallery levels. The accounts survive among the records of royal administration in the Public Record Office because in 1240 Henry III took over responsibility for the organization and much of the funding of the chapel works. The Abbey's own funds were evidently insufficient, and when a papal bull was issued in 1245 it was noted that the monks had begun the church 'in so sumptuous a fashion that they became unable to complete it from their own resources'. The implication here seems to be that the Chapel was thought of as only the first stage of a completely new abbey church. Though this may have been the intention in 1245, it is clear that the great church which actually began to rise from the ground in 1246 was conceived on a grander scale than the Lady Chapel, for in 1256 the vault and upper walls of the latter had to be pulled down and rebuilt higher to make them harmonize with the new work to which they were by then being joined. The Lady Chapel of 1220-45 was thus a self-contained project, one of a considerable number of such chapels added to the east ends of major English Romanesque churches in the late twelfth and early thirteenth centuries. The positioning of these chapels on main axes made them function as symbols of the central place in Christian devotion which the cult of the Virgin had then attained.

The King's contribution to the Lady Chapel works between 1240 and 1245 amounted to around £200, a substantial sum but not an immoderate one given the special status of the Abbey and its location next to the principal royal palace of England. This relatively modest involvement in no way anticipates Henry's momentous decision to rebuild the entire church at his own expense. Support for church building was *de rigueur* for medieval kings, but no other European ruler ever bore the entire cost of a great Gothic church of cathedral scale.

The motives behind this uniquely lavish act of artistic patronage have to be sought in the king's religious and political objectives. The contemporary historian Matthew Paris singled out Henry's devotion to the Confessor, which had in fact been assuming physical form since 1241, when work began on the precious metal and jewelled shrine for the Saint's relics. Even by medieval standards, Henry III was exceptionally pious — he is reputed to have heard mass several times each day — but besides being a symptom of his piety, the cult of St Edward was for him an integral part of a cult of kingship which he had been developing from the 1230s with the aim of gaining acceptance for his quasi-priestly and 'absolutist' conception of monarchy. As the setting for the coronation of every king of England from the Conqueror onwards, Westminster Abbey was the royal church *par excellence*, and by reconstructing it Henry was in effect refashioning the image of the English monarchy. It seems unlikely that he would have seen any irony in the fact that his emulating St Edward's rebuilding of the church resulted in the destruction of this chief product of the Confessor's piety. Henry's robust and unselfconscious (and typically medieval) approach to the revitalization of religious tradition showed itself also in his commissioning of a new and topically slanted version of the *'Life and Miracles of St Edward'*. After his enshrined bones, the most important relics of the Confessor were not his buildings but his crown, sceptre and staff, the principal items of the regalia used at each coronation.

The timing of the decision to rebuild is interesting. Henry's claim to be God's vicar and lord of all men in his realm, clergy as well as laity, had been arousing stiff opposition from bishops and barons alike during the decade before 1245, but towards the end of that year, only a few months after work began on the demolition of the Confessor's church, Bishop Grosseteste of Lincoln, the leading English intellectual of his day, wrote to Henry that the sacrament of anointing a king

The nave, crossing and north transept, looking north-west.

at his coronation 'by no means places the royal dignity above or on a level with the priestly'. Grosseteste was made to apologize, but the challenge posed by such opinions must have helped spur Henry into rebuilding the coronation church and royal shrine-house with a splendour intended to outshine all other English churches.

Another incentive to begin rebuilding Westminster Abbey in 1245 was rivalry with the kings of France. During Henry's lifetime the French Crown had overtaken the English Crown in power, prestige and wealth, and Henry can hardly have failed to become aware that the churches most intimately associated with the Capetian Kings were in process of being built or rebuilt as splendid examples of the Gothic style pioneered in northern France. The eastern parts of Reims Cathedral, the coronation church, were inaugurated in 1241 after thirty years' work, and the remodelling of the abbey church of St-Denis, the royal necropolis and repository for the coronation regalia, had been proceeding steadily since 1231. Both these great churches were initiated by and for the clergy who served them, but Louis IX had assumed personal responsibility for two churches of lesser scope, the Cistercian Abbey of Royaumont, some 30km (19 miles) north of Paris (begun c. 1228) and the Sainte-Chapelle, the main chapel in the French equivalent to Westminster Palace (begun c. 1241-3). Royaumont's conformity to the standards of austerity appropriate to a Cistercian church made it less influential on Westminster than the sumptuously finished Sainte-Chapelle, whose centrepiece, the relic of the Crown of Thorns, was calculated to glorify the Crown of France.

Henry III's new church was to combine in a single building the functions of Reims, St-Denis and the Sainte-Chapelle. To the established roles of coronation church, shrine and repository for the regalia, Henry added two more. By 1246 he had decided to be buried near St Edward rather than in the choir of the London Temple Church: the intention was clearly to inaugurate an English royal pantheon comparable to that which had long existed at St-Denis. In 1247 Henry obtained from the Patriarch of Jerusalem the relic of the Precious Blood of Christ, which he bore to the Abbey in a solemn procession intended to recall those which had marked Louis' reception of the Crown of Thorns and other relics of Christ's Passion in 1239 and 1241.

Westminster's architectural debts to Reims, the Sainte-Chapelle and other French churches are discussed below; here it is enough to note that they add up to England's closest approximation to a thirteenth-century French cathedral. The fundamental foreignness of the building can be seen as reflecting Henry III's remoteness from the nationalistic outlook of many of his subjects and also his eagerness to cut a great figure on the international political stage. In 1245 he had not yet seen for himself any major work of French Gothic architecture, and so may not have realized how far Westminster Abbey was from being a French design transplanted to English soil. If, on the other hand, Henry was aware that much of the detail was English, the possibility arises that the Abbey was consciously conceived as an amalgam of French and English traditions paralleling the carefully cultivated binational character of the Court and the royal administration. In its relative Englishness, Westminster contrasts strikingly with the only other mid-thirteenth-century instances of the exportation of the French cathedral formula, León in Castille, Cologne in the Rhineland and Strassburg in Alsace. All these churches are purely French in style and make no concessions to the undeveloped versions of Gothic current in their respective regions. Whether or not the traditional English elements in the design at Westminster are the result of deliberate choice on the part of the king, they testify to the vigour of early thirteenth-century English architecture, the most productive and highly evolved national tradition of Gothic outside France.

Whereas the French format of the Abbey has to be ascribed to the King's intervention, the detailed designing was in the hands of an architect known in his lifetime simply as 'Henry' or 'Master Henry'. After his death in 1253 he was referred to once as 'Henry of Reyns', and his son Hugh also used this surname. Given that Westminster owes particularly much to Reims Cathedral (see pp. 41-2), it would be an extraordinary coincidence if Henry's name derived not from Reims but from the only English placename spelt 'Reyns', Rayne in Essex.

So what was the nature of Henry's connection with Reims? The only evidence on which to base an answer is the fabric itself, and this, to anticipate pp. 39, 59 and 64, shows clearly the imprint of a mind unfamiliar with some of the more technical aspects of French Gothic and at the same time ready to countenance what would have been regarded as solecisms on the other side of the Channel. A French-trained architect could conceivably have been involved in the designing of Westminster if his role had been confined to providing small-scale drawings and if the work of translating the drawings into architecture had been left to English executant masons. However, this hypothesis does not square with what is known of contemporary procedure or with the documentary evidence that Henry of Reyns was present at Westminster more or less continuously.

Just how Henry had acquired his knowledge of recent French

churches will never be known. In the mid-thirteenth century, drawings were beginning to circulate around the most important cathedral lodges of north-western Europe, and it is possible, though not provable, that there existed some mechanism for the long-distance transmission of architectural ideas which obviated travel by architects. And yet, on balance, it seems most likely that Henry had personally visited Reims and the other major French sites, whether as a young journeyman or as a fully fledged master gleaning information prior to drawing up the designs for Westminster. The building itself suggests either that he remained defiantly impervious to some of the procedures evolved in the north French lodges or, more probably, that he did not have the entrée to the lodges and was obliged to make sense of what he saw as best he could. So the evidential significance of Henry's surname remains a mystery, since there appears to be no parallel for a mason's adopting a name merely on the strength of a visit. Might it even have started as a private nickname? Its absence from the official records kept during his lifetime could be interpreted in this way, although Henry was of course too important a figure at Westminster to need further identification.

Westminster Abbey was not the first commission to Henry from his royal namesake. In 1240 he began work on a splendid set of royal apartments in the lower bailey of Windsor Castle, the most important feature of which was a large chapel dedicated to St Edward. The small fraction of this chapel to have survived later rebuilding reveals influence from Reims Cathedral, so it is inherently likely that·its destroyed windows incorporated the bar tracery invented at Reims and used throughout the church and monastic offices at Westminster. Positive evidence that the Windsor chapel did indeed pre-empt Westminster in the use of tracery is the reference to a circular cusped opening in the record of repairs made to the glazing after a storm in 1295.

Binham Priory in Norfolk has a west front with three traceried windows, which Matthew Paris states was completed during the time of a prior whose rule ended in 1244. Some scholars have been reluctant to accept this dating, suggesting either that Paris was mistaken, or that the central window, the most advanced stylistically, was inserted later on. However, Paris's testimony must stand, for as a monk of St Albans Abbey, the mother house of Binham, he was well placed to obtain accurate information. Moreover, various kinds of bar tracery are used throughout the façade, not only in the central window. Since the side windows at Binham are modelled on the interior of the main apse at Reims and the moulding profiles have close parallels at Westminster, we may be dealing once more with an early work of

Henry of Reyns. Binham is, of course, not where one would expect to find architecture of a kind otherwise unknown in the 1240s outside the Royal Works, but the incongruity is lessened by the link with St Albans, where the king stayed often on journeys north of London. So Westminster cannot be regarded as the first English building to incorporate fully developed bar-tracery. This title must be shared by Windsor and Binham since there is insufficient evidence to decide absolute priority. But neither Windsor nor Binham was much in the public eye, and there can be little doubt that it was Westminster Abbey which drew the attention of the whole country to this novel extension of the vocabulary of Gothic architecture.

Henry of Reyns had died or retired before 1253, when his place was taken by John of Gloucester. Of the detailed account rolls which once existed, only that for 1253 still survives, and by correlating its references to the fabric with the evidence for the building sequence contained in the fabric itself it is possible to gain a good idea of how far the church had progressed when its original designer disappeared from the scene. Construction followed the general east-west sequence usual in great medieval churches, with low outer walls preceding the high walls of the main vessels. At the west end of the eastern arm, the high walls were not quite finished, so the high vaults had probably not been begun. In the transepts, the outer walls were well advanced, for the accounts mention lead roofing laid on the north transept portals as well as the construction of the east walk of the cloister, which was integral with the west aisle of the south transept. The high east wall of the south transept had risen at least to arcade level. The completion of the transepts appears to have been marked by the king's order in June 1259 that the eastern parts of the Romanesque nave be demolished and rebuilt to match the new work further east. The instruction in the same document that the altars in the transepts (*aliis*) be constructed (*reparari*) suggests that this part of the church had only just been finished.

John of Gloucester died in the summer or autumn of 1260. Most of his work adhered to Henry of Reyns' original conception, but in the nave he felt free to make important revisions, mostly in the direction of increased richness. Under his successor, Robert of Beverley, there were again changes, but of lesser importance. Work was now proceeding much more slowly and when the king died in 1272 the only parts of the nave completed and usable were the five eastern bays, those housing the choir stalls of the monks. The climax to nearly a quarter-century of work had come on 13 October 1269, when St Edward's relics were translated into the costly shrine Henry had prepared for them and mass was celebrated for the first time in the new east end. At this point, the eastern nave bays were probably covered by a temporary roof, as the £3,000 laid out on the fabric between the translation and the cessation of work in 1272 must have been spent largely on the upper walls, vault and outer roof. No doubt Henry would have wished to complete everything in his own lifetime, but he may have drawn comfort from the fact that the proportion of his church built before 1272 was equivalent to that achieved by the Confessor before his death in 1066.

The building and decoration of Westminster Abbey was a complex financial operation controlled by a special exchequer which until 1264 had independence from the main Exchequer, the central accounting department of the royal administration. The Westminster exchequer was not a wholly new organization but a revamping of one which had existed since the beginning of the reign to administer building work at Westminster Palace. At its head were the keeper of the works and his associates, the architect (master mason) and a representative of the Abbey. Other men, including the master carpenter, served as associate keepers for short periods. The money spent came only partly from the royal treasury. Much more derived from fines and other financial obligations to the Crown, the collection of which could be a considerable burden on the keepers. From c. 1250 Henry III's finances deteriorated steadily, and occasionally the money ran out altogether.

The keeper of the works at Westminster from 1240 was a royal clerk, Edward, appropriately known as 'of Westminster' since he was there almost continuously. Edward had been brought up in the royal court and inherited the keepership and the office of melter to the Exchequer from his father Odo who was almost certainly a practising goldsmith. His knowledge of goldsmith's work made him the almost inevitable choice as 'keeper of the works of the shrine of St Edward', when this project was begun in 1241. Far from being a faceless functionary, Edward was the instrument of the king's will in everything touching pious benefactions and artistic patronage. He was not only a valued financial expert but the interpreter of the king's wishes in things ranging from the feeding of ten thousand paupers to the purchase of a crown for the king of Norway. On at least two occasions Henry accepted his advice on artistic matters. The successful prosecution of the works at Westminster must have owed much to this busy and resourceful man whom the king often addressed as his 'beloved clerk'. After Edward retired from his keeperships in 1263 or 1264, the Westminster works were by stages brought under the control of the central Exchequer, a reflection both of the reduced scale of spending and the lesser status of Edward's successor in the eyes of the king.

The craftsmen who actually made the building were in eight categories: white cutters (masons who worked freestone), marblers (who worked Purbeck marble), layers or setters (who set in position the stones cut by white cutters and marblers), carpenters, polishers (of the marble), smiths, glaziers and plumbers. Labourers assisted all the former, and when foundations were being dug there would be diggers also. The detailed accounts for 1253 show that the workforce averaged three hundred men, rising to over four hundred for three weeks in June and July and dropping to a hundred in the second week of November. The presence of master masons working under Master Henry and his successors is an indication of the scale of operations, for normally a major project would be headed by only one master. Unfortunately, the rates of pay of the different kinds and grades of craftsmen are not recorded.

The cost of building at Westminster between 1246 and 1272 has been calculated as £41,248 and the cost of the shrine was between £4,000 and £5,000. It is impossible to give a meaningful modern equivalent for the huge total of £45,000 plus, but if one allows for the smallness of the thirteenth-century economy relative to ours, the figure would have to be reckoned in billions. Some sense of the scale of the cost is given by the thirteenth-century building labourer's daily wage of one and a half pence and by Henry III's average normal annual income of around £34-35,000. The cost of the Sainte-Chapelle, including its stained glass and sculpture, though not its shrine, was estimated at over £40,000 tournois (roughly £13,000 stirling), but this figure may be rather high as it comes from an adulatory memoir written for the French royal family after Louis IX's canonization in 1297. The presbytery of Ely Cathedral, built between 1234 and 1250, and lavishly ornamented by any normal standard, cost £5,040 18s 7d or, very roughly, about £700 per bay. At Westminster each bay must have cost well over twice as much, and there can be little doubt that the unit cost thus reckoned exceeded that of every other thirteenth-century church in Europe. Only the nave of York Minster, begun in 1291, is comparable in its combination of French scale and English elaboration.

The influence of Westminster Abbey on subsequent English architecture was very considerable, though less than might be expected. The French format of the building was imitated only at two abbeys which were in different senses royal: Hailes in Gloucestershire and Battle in Sussex, and even here the imitation appears to have been confined to the ground plan of the east end. Most major church building projects initiated in England during the later thirteenth century were in the nature of additions to older fabrics, so

Westminster's height and tall proportions could not readily be reproduced; but the general lack of interest in the ground plan suggests that this aspect of Westminster smacked too much of Henry III's supranational outlook and unrealistically elevated view of his kingly vocation. The innovatory aspect of the Abbey which gained immediate acceptance was window tracery: hereafter, no important new building in England was without this feature. Over and above individual motifs, Westminster's significance in the history of architectural style is that it ended the insularity of early thirteenth-century English Gothic and inaugurated a period of roughly fifty years during which the English were receptive to at least some aspects of French architecture. In the history of patronage it marks the emergence of the Royal Works as England's pre-eminent centre of architectural excellence, a position it was to hold for many centuries, albeit with some interruptions.

THE COMPLETION OF THE NAVE

The death of Henry III in 1272 brought work on the nave to an abrupt halt. Edward I felt no obligation to continue funding the church of the saint from whom he took his name, despite the injunction to do so in his father's will. The thirteenth-century work ended at clearstorey sill level in the fifth bay of the nave, to the west of which seven bays of the Confessor's nave were left standing. The contrast between the old and new parts of the nave must have been stark indeed, a challenge to the piety and pride of later generations. As it turned out, no late medieval king was to emulate Henry III's generosity, so the monks themselves had to find most of the money for the continuation. Of some £21,000 spent before 1534, no more than £6,065 was given by royalty: £1,685 by Richard II, £3,861 by Henry V and £519 from Edward IV and his family.

The monastic offices were severely damaged by fire in 1298, a disaster which removed any prospect of completing Henry III's work in the foreseeable future. From 1335 there existed a special New Work fund ostensibly for rebuilding necessitated by the 1298 fire, and in 1341-3 this was being applied to repairing the eleventh-century part of the nave. These works, which were already in progress under the aegis of the sacrist in 1338, amounted to a thorough refurbishing intended to make the nave serviceable for some time to come. From 1344 the New Work income was applied to rebuilding the monastic offices and abbot's house, and only in 1387 did it become available for the continuation of Henry III's nave. This project had been revived in

1375, almost certainly at the instigation of Cardinal Langham, abbot of Westminster from 1349 to 1362. Letters of 1375 and 1376 reveal Langham's impatience with the obstructive attitude of his successor as abbot, Nicholas Litlyngton (1362-86), whose main priority was the completion of the monastic offices. However, Litlyngton could not afford to offend the wealthy Langham, whose gifts in his lifetime are said to have amounted to about £3,000 and whose will made the abbey his residuary legatee. Litlyngton therefore ordered the demolition of the wall between the cloister and south aisle of the old nave and laid the foundation stone of the new nave on 3 March 1376. It is difficult not to conclude that Litlyngton's compliance was only given because the new section of nave wall was necessary in order to finish the cloisters, which had stood otherwise complete for ten years. During the rest of Litlyngton's abbacy work on the nave advanced at a snail's pace. Records of payments for iron window bars show that the outer walls of the aisles were in hand, but it is unlikely that work had reached the two westernmost bays, whose building would inevitably disrupt life in the fine abbot's house that Litlyngton had built.

The design of the nave aisle walls can safely be attributed to John Palterton, master mason to the Abbey from 1344 until 1376-7 and possibly until 1378-9. The building of the main arcades of the nave was not begun until 1387-8, but the aisle walls show that the most remarkable thing about the nave design had been settled by 1376, that is its careful imitation of the thirteenth-century work. This departure from the usual medieval practice of employing a modern style when adding to older work has sometimes been regarded as an early instance of English conservatism, and the near-parallel provided by the fourteenth-century nave at Beverley Minster adds some weight to this interpretation. However, neither Westminster nor Beverley can show such strict adherence to a thirteenth-century design as the fourteenth- and fifteenth-century parts of Châlons-sur-Marne Cathedral, where virtually everything except the foliage carving is a faithful copy. The main incentive to keep Gothic modernism at bay at all three places must have been the relatively unusual situation of thirteenth-century work being broken off part way along the nave. If the old work had not turned the corner from the transepts there would have been a much less good case for rejecting the current architectural idiom.

The nave continuation was put on a new footing when it became the sole beneficiary of the New Work fund in 1387. The initiative behind this fresh start seems to have come from Richard II, who, on declaring himself to be of age, promised an annual subsidy of £100. The royal architect Henry Yeveley was appointed at a retaining fee of

The interior, looking west from the choir screen.

£5 a year plus expenses. Unlike Palterton, whose career was spent almost entirely in abbey service, Yeveley was the leading architect of his day with a huge private practice as well as his Royal Works post. His role at Westminster was essentially that of a consultant, present as and when the nature of the work in hand required it. The changes in the inherited designs which can reasonably be ascribed to him are discussed on p. 69. Yeveley died in 1400, by which time the aisle walls and most of the arcades were finished, together with the corresponding level of the west front, the only part of the nave where he was free to employ the Perpendicular style.

Richard II's deposition and death in 1399 were a great setback for the nave works, to which he had intended to bequeath the residue of his jewels. In 1404 work ground to a halt once more, and nothing was done until Henry V, shocked by the condition of the nave at his coronation, promised 1,000 marks a year. At Henry's death in 1422 the gallery was complete and the clearstorey had been begun. Throughout his son's reign, the nave works languished, like so many other building projects, although they never stopped completely. With the appointment of Thomas Mylling as Keeper of the New Work in 1467, activity increased again. The fifth bay, whose clearstorey must have been finished in Henry V's time, was roofed in 1469. The clearstorey of bays six to eleven was finished next and their roof was erected in 1474-9. The flying buttresses were built in advance of the vault, in 1477-83, and by 1490 the vault over bays seven to eleven was in place. The west towers and the bay between them had probably risen no higher than the gallery, the level they had reached by 1422. Preparations for the aisle-level vaults inside the towers were being made in 1490, the great west window and the clearstorey windows looking into the towers were finished in 1496, and the high vaults here and over bays five and six were built in 1504-6. A final burst of activity in 1528-34 brought the north-west tower up to the level of the clearstorey walls. The cessation of work on the west front ordered by the last pre-Dissolution abbot, a Peterborough monk intruded by Thomas Cromwell, must have seemed at the time a sure sign that the end of the monastery was near.

The Dissolution was finally effected in January 1540, and during the next two decades the monks were succeeded by no fewer than four different régimes, none of them in a position to continue the work abandoned in 1534. In December 1540 the church became the cathedral of a new diocese of Westminster carved out of the London diocese; ten years afterwards the bishopric was suppressed and the Abbey made the cathedral of London jointly with St Paul's. From 1541 the monastic offices were either demolished or converted into houses for the members of the cathedral chapter and their servants, changes which cannot have been wholly reversed during Queen Mary's short-lived restoration of the monastery (September 1556-July 1559). On 21 May 1560 Queen Elizabeth vested possession in the College of St Peter, Westminster, and it is this body which still shoulders the heavy responsibility of maintaining the fabric.

THE RESTORATIONS

In choosing Reigate stone as the main building material of the Abbey, the medieval masons created an enormous problem for subsequent generations. Reigate, a greenish-grey calcareous sandstone, has such poor weathering qualities that it is not now used for any important purpose. Atmospheric pollution was presumably not a serious problem in thirteenth-century Westminster, but by the early eighteenth-century domestic coal burning had brought about the decay of external stonework to a depth of four inches (10cm) in places. Renewal of the exterior has been in progress almost continuously from 1660, and in the major restoration proceeding at the time of writing (1985) many parts of the building are being refaced for the third time. The great variety of stones substituted for Reigate during the last three centuries has become more obvious than ever since the cleaning programme initiated in 1973, yet the effect is less disturbing than might have been expected.

Henry III's work was in need of restoration long before the nave reached completion. In 1373-80 the pinnacles, parapets and window tracery of the church and chapter house were undergoing renovation, and between 1451 and 1480 the rose, gable and pinnacles of the south transept were replaced and the flying buttresses of the apse rebuilt. Information about restorations between the Dissolution and the 1690s is very hard to come by. A reference in 1580 to a bricklayer stopping up six large windows which had become decayed hints at an escalating problem and the inability of a relatively impecunious chapter to deal with it effectively. Dean Andrewes (1601-5) created a restoration fund and Dean Williams (1620-44) personally paid £4,500 for refacing work on the north side of the nave and for placing statues in hitherto unfilled niches on the buttresses. In 1662 a more urgent campaign of repair began; the high vault of the eastern arm was said at this time to be in danger of collapse. The late seventeenth-century marked a general nadir in the appreciation of Gothic, and most of the work done c. 1662-98 involved paring down and simplifying details, the north transept front being the main victim of this procedure. On the credit side is the careful renewal of the south rose around 1670. The Abbey Surveyor from 1662 to 1675 was Edward Woodroffe, Assistant Surveyor to Wren at St Paul's.

A new chapter in the history of the restorations opened in 1698 when part of the coal tax which financed the rebuilding of St Paul's was made available for repairing the Abbey. The exterior of the eastern arm and transepts received much attention, as in the preceding decades, and by 1710 the eastern half of the south side of the nave had been refaced. Wren wrote to the Dean in 1713 recommending that a Gothic steeple be built over the crossing, the aim being to endow the skyline of western London with an ornament comparable to the dome of St Paul's. A wooden model of the spire was finished in 1716 and Wren's deputy, William Dickinson, continued making designs until 1724. The present stump of a tower was built in 1725-7. This desire to enhance the Gothic character of the Abbey was fulfilled in the case of the north transept façade, which was refaced and regothicized between 1719 and 1722 in accordance with Dickinson's designs of 1713. The coal tax money came to an end in 1728 and in 1731 a fresh Parliamentary grant was obtained for the completion of the west front to the designs of Nicholas Hawksmoor, Wren's successor as Surveyor. Work lasted from 1734 to 1745.

In 1803 fire destroyed the roof and vault of the crossing tower. James Wyatt, dubbed 'the destroyer' for his cavalier restorations of Durham, Salisbury and Hereford, reinstated a vault like that burned except that it was made of Bernasconi's composition painted to simulate the colour and jointing of masonry. In the restoration of the exterior of Henry VII's Chapel, begun in 1809, an infinitely more serious attitude to Gothic was imposed on Wyatt by a Parliamentary committee influenced by the preservationist views of antiquarians such as Richard Gough and John Carter.

To the Abbey surveyors of the Victorian period the seventeenth- and eighteenth-century alterations to Henry III's church were both an affront and an opportunity to recreate the original design. This interventionist policy was implemented first in Edward Blore's restoration of the north side of the nave in 1837-49, and was developed during the long surveyorship of (Sir) George Gilbert Scott, from 1849 to 1878. The clearstoreys, south transept gable and, most importantly, the north transept portals were all returned to what Scott considered to have been their thirteenth-century state. Where the archaeological evidence for original forms was lacking, Scott's knowledge of period precedent took over. Unfortunately he kept his archaeological cards very close to his chest, and by failing to keep any records of his discoveries he left himself open to accusations of finding what he wanted to find and restoring in accordance with his own aesthetic preferences.

The north transept portals, Scott's self-confessed 'labour of love', were begun in 1875 and completed in 1878-85 by his son Oldrid Scott. The upper parts of the façade were recreated between 1884 and 1892 by J L Pearson, a distinguished Victorian Goth with vastly less experience of restoration than Scott. Pearson's work was done in great secrecy, and when unveiled in 1892, was greeted by a chorus of protest led by William Morris. This *cause célèbre* greatly advanced general acceptance of the 'anti-scrape' tenets preached by Morris from 1877 onwards. The next two surveyors, J T Micklethwaite (1898-1906) and W R Lethaby (1902-28) were both exponents of Morris's principles and both published scholarly works on the medieval architecture of the Abbey. Scott's only important change in the interior had been the 'induration' of the stonework with shellac in the hope of hardening the crumbling surface and protecting it from the acid atmosphere of Victorian London. The only uncontested consequence of this process was to darken the stone. The shellac was cleaned off between 1953 and 1964. Lightening of the interior had begun in 1932 with the limewashing of Henry VII's Chapel. In the early 1960s the nave and south transept roofs were renewed, without any record being made of their previous state. The current programme of external refacing began in 1974, and at the time of writing only the west front and the adjoining six west bays on the south side of the nave remain to be treated.

THE LAYOUT OF HENRY III'S CHURCH

The need to incorporate the barely completed Lady Chapel made the task of planning the new building much less straightforward than it would have otherwise. The basic problem was the restricted space available between the chapel and the east side of the cloister. This could not reasonably be rebuilt farther west without reducing the area of the cloister garth or rebuilding all the offices bordering it, both options doubtless unacceptable to the monks, whose communal life had to continue on the site. The elements which it was necessary somehow to accommodate between the Lady Chapel and the east wall of the cloister were the ambulatory, the chapel containing the Confessor's shrine, the sanctuary and the transept with its east and west aisles. The sanctuary could not take in part of the crossing as this would be needed at future coronations for the stage supporting the throne.

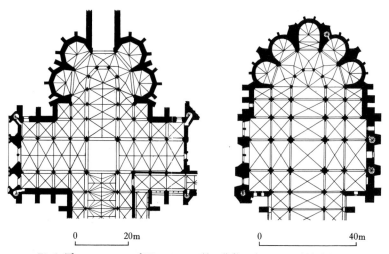

0   20m   0   40m

Fig 1: The eastern parts of Westminster Abbey (left) and Reims Cathedral (right).

The solution to this problem of restricted length was to fit the east walk of the cloister within the space which otherwise would have been occupied entirely by the west aisle of the south transept. Above the cloister a space opening into the church and matching the upper parts of the other aisles created the illusion of a west aisle blocked by high screens. The inspiration for this ingenious solution probably came from the destroyed abbey of Beaulieu, Hampshire, founded by King John in 1204 and consecrated in 1246 in Henry's presence. The west aisle at Beaulieu was omitted in order to make way for the cloister but it is not known if there was a dummy aisle overhead. The same arrangement existed at Beaulieu's Cistercian sister Royaumont, built for Louis IX.

The other main design problem arising from the retention of the Lady Chapel concerned the planning of the apse, ambulatory and radiating chapels. Small fragments of the Lady Chapel surviving at the west end of Henry VII's Chapel show that it was around 8.3m (27ft) wide, as wide as each radiating chapel at Reims. Henry of Reyns decided to give all the other radiating chapels the same width as the Lady Chapel, a normal feature of French east ends and unavoidable except by making the central openings of the apse wider than the rest or by disrupting the radial arrangement of vault ribs and buttresses. Like Reims, Westminster has five radiating chapels, but imitation of the half-decagonal layout of Reims was impracticable, as a decagon with 8.3m (27ft) sides would have resulted in main vessels with a span of about 13m (43ft). There was simply not the room for this at Westminster: the transepts, for example, would have extended so far

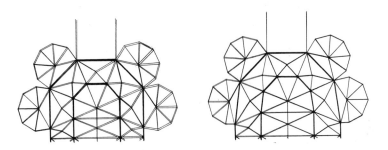

LEFT: Fig 2: The layout of the east end as if based on a regular octagon, and RIGHT: Fig. 3: as actually built.

east from the cloister as to make the eastern arm too short to contain both the sanctuary and the Confessor's Chapel.

Henry of Reyns' way out of this impasse was to make the side aisles much narrower than they are at Reims and to plan the apse as five sides of an octagon, each side 8.3m (27ft) long. Used without modification, this scheme would have made the entrance arches of the two western radiating chapels parallel to the longitudinal axis (fig. 2), rather than at an angle, as French tradition required. To avoid this solecism, Henry opened out the 'mouth' of his part-octagon so that it equalled the width of the basic octagon as measured from angle to angle (fig. 3). The residual shortcomings of this solution affect only the lower level of the east end: the radiating chapels are abnormally large in relation to the main apse and extend much further westwards than it does; instead of rectangular chapels opening out of the irregular easternmost aisle bays there are only huge buttresses; the symmetry of the two western radiating chapels is upset by planning them as if they adjoined a regularly octagonal ambulatory and then placing the western jambs of their entrance arches in accordance with the irregular layout actually adopted (fig. 3). None of these peculiarities occurs in contemporary French churches, nor does the plan of the radiating chapels — six sides of a nonagon. What the attraction of the nonagons was, is unclear, for they led to yet another departure from convention, the presence of an angle rather than a window on the central axis of each chapel. It looks as if the main concern was to fit in four windows per chapel instead of the usual three. In the main vessel of the eastern arm the most important consequence of Henry's geometrical juggling is that the sides of the apse are nearly as wide as those of the rectangular bays. Less satisfactory is the eccentric positioning of the shafts on the western apse piers and the high vault shafts which rise above them.

A TOUR OF THE EXTERIOR

The East End

The tour begins with the east end and the east side of the south transept and continues in an anticlockwise direction. For the exteriors of
the monastic offices and Henry VII's Chapel see pp. 87-8 and 71-3
respectively. Apart from Henry VII's Chapel and the west front,
inspection of the exterior from close quarters is not a specially
pleasurable experience. The refacing work of the seventeenth and
eighteenth centuries entailed such drastic simplifications of detail that
the effect is almost as if a model has been enlarged to full size. The
mechanical finish of the masonry, now mostly nineteenth- and
twentieth-century re-replacement, accentuates this effect. Particularly lame are the obelisk pinnacles and the acorn-like corbels
supplanting shafts on the window mullions. The restoration of the
1970s replicated all pre-existing features except Blore's and Scott's
quatrefoil parapet, which was replaced by crenellations.

The French-inspired height and tall proportions of the Abbey
register immediately as exceptional among English medieval
churches. The distance between the apex of the clearstorey windows
and the ambulatory floor is around 31.7m (104ft), as against 38m
(125ft) at Reims. The main reason for the disparity must be the rather
restricted span of the main vessels; and one can only speculate
whether, given an unencumbered site, the height would have risen to
a French dimension. Hawksmoor's dumpy crossing tower is at least a
reminder of the original intention to have a proper lantern tower, a
feature which the French had found impossible to combine safely
with main walls more than 35m (114ft) high. The main concomitant
of Westminster's height is the great array of flying buttresses, the only
example in England of the two tiers of flyers normal in French High
Gothic. The pinnacles overtop the clearstorey, as at Reims, but the
flyers are far steeper in pitch and hence more efficient as abutments to
the high vaults than those of any French High Gothic cathedral except Bourges. According to recent technical analyses of French
flying buttresses, the upper tier exists mainly to transmit the thrusts
exerted by wind pressure on the high, steeply pitched roof.

The tall clearstorey and the flyers are quite difficult to see from the
ground thanks to the huge size of the radiating chapels and also to the
high outer walls of the galleries. Galleries seem such an anachronism
in a mid-thirteenth-century church as to demand some special
explanation. The Confessor's Abbey, like many Romanesque
churches in England, had galleries, and it will be suggested below
(p.62) that they were used for a purpose which remained valid after

The Abbey looking north-east, from the Victoria Tower of the Palace of Westminster.

Henry III's rebuilding. The choirs at Canterbury and Lincoln were two prestigious and relatively recent English buildings which had galleries lit by ranges of low lancet windows. Instead of lancets, Henry of Reyns used a type of tracery window devised in France specially for situations where restrictions on height ruled out windows of the usual upright format. These strange convex-sided triangles were first used in the west front of Amiens Cathedral *c.* 1225-30 and were copied in the lower chapel of the Sainte-Chapelle. In their overall proportions the Westminster windows are closer to Amiens, but awareness of the Sainte-Chapelle is evident from the detailing and from the use of small two-light windows in the narrow bays of the gallery, just as in the narrow compartments of the apse of the Parisian building. The Sainte-Chapelle was begun no more than four years before Westminster, and it seems very likely that Henry had been sent to study this supreme product of Louis IX's patronage. A feature of Henry's own devising is the obtusely pointed arch framing each convex triangle. In the north transept of Hereford Cathedral, built in the 1260s by Henry III's close advisor Peter of Aigueblanche, these strange arches become the leading motif of the design.

Modern French sources like the Sainte-Chapelle contributed far

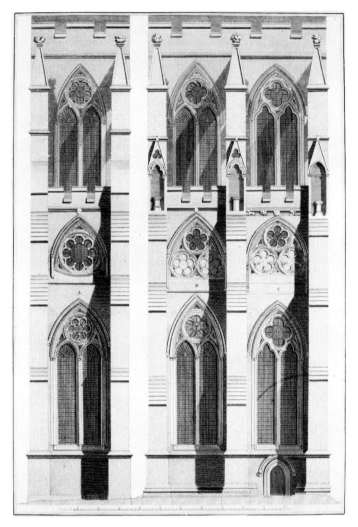

*Exterior elevations of the eastern arm (left) and the north side of the nave (right) from
Neale's History and Antiquities of Westminster Abbey, volume 2 (1823).*

less to the Abbey as a whole than the outdated but ideologically rele-
vant Reims. The fundamental importance of Reims as a source is clear
from the use of two-light-and-encircled-sexfoil windows throughout
the clearstorey, aisles and chapels. If the prime consideration had
been to appear abreast of the French fashions of 1245, the clearstorey
would have incorporated four-light windows such as those used in the
chapter house at Westminster. The archaic aspect of the tracery

design is hardly mitigated by modern details like the merging of the roll mouldings of the circle and lancet heads, the foliate cusps of the lower windows and the largeness of the component pieces of stone.

Crenellations would be surprising things to find on a great church had they not become so common in later medieval English architecture. If they are an original feature and not an innovation made during the late fourteenth-century repairs, they rank as the earliest crenellations on a major English church, with those at Exeter Cathedral, begun in 1279, the next earliest. It is not clear whether the intention was to evoke the battlements of the Heavenly Jerusalem or simply to give the church the same modishly martial trim as was used on so many of Henry III's buildings at Westminster and other palaces. The only individual feature of the east side of the south transept calling for special mention is the door in the southernmost bay, the king's private entrance from the palace. The head of this door has a curious type of arch much favoured at Westminster, though not invented here, a very depressed pointed arch with short vertical pieces immediately over the capitals. On the north side of the eastern arm, the only non-regular features are the Perpendicular window inserted to light Abbot Islip's chantry and, on the east side of the north transept, another small door, possibly also intended for royal use, with some remains of thirteenth-century carving on its head.

The North Transept Front

The north transept façade was the main ceremonial entrance to the Abbey before the completion of the nave in the early sixteenth-century. As the front which faced towards London and was most accessible from the palace, it received the ambitious treatment normally reserved for west fronts. Its combination of richness and prominence in the public eye proved its undoing. In the early 1660s the stonework had become so desperately decayed that the Chapter felt impelled to order repairs, yet neither they nor their surveyor Edward Woodroffe acknowledged any need to perpetuate the unfashionable Gothic complexities of the original design. Comparison of fig. 4 with the right-hand part of fig. 5 makes clear that Woodroffe's work was the merest butchery.

As well as cropping gables and hacking out tracery Woodroffe completely demolished the chapel-cum-porch added to the central portal *c.* 1358-62. No doubt the main aim was to get rid of what had become a financial liability. By 1713 the tide had turned and William Dickinson had designed a scheme for regothicizing the front (left-hand part of fig. 5). This was executed with some variations in

LEFT: Fig 4: Etching by Wenceslaus Hollar, 1654, from Dugdale's Monasticon Anglicanum.
RIGHT: Fig 5: Drawing by William Dickinson before 1713, showing (right) pre-existing work and (left) proposed alterations (Westminster Abbey Library).

1719-22. Dickinson had no compunction about improving the thirteenth-century design. Anachronistically detailed niches, parapets and pinnacles were introduced where the old work was thought insufficiently rich; two major original elements, the rose and the tympanum over the central portal (fig. 6), were altered; and some post-medieval modifications were retained and embellished, notably the enclosed staircases on top of the uppermost flying buttresses and the horizontal wall above and between the portals.

Tragically, Dickinson's drawing was in a private collection and unknown to Scott when the portals were reconstructed to his designs from 1875 onwards. The remains of original work and the engraving by Hollar were his guides, and had the Dickinson drawing been available he would probably not have put Lincoln-derived canopies over the image pedestals or have made the central tympanum an orthodox French affair with horizontal bands of figure sculpture. Unlike Scott,

44

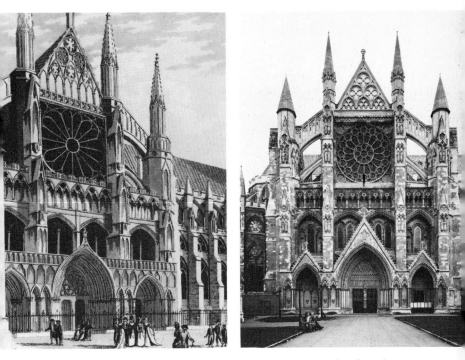

LEFT: Fig 6: Detail of aquatint from Thomas Malton's A Picturesque Tour through London and Westminster, 1793. RIGHT: Fig 7: The front as in 1986.

who at least acted in good faith, Pearson obstinately adhered to the designs he had formulated before the publication of the Dickinson drawing in 1884. Basically, Pearson's approach was to translate the façade as he found it into a 'correct' thirteenth-century manner and to base the detailing of his gable, rose and gallery on the Hollar engraving, where these features appear only about 5cm (2in) high. The result is both a travesty of the thirteenth-century design and the worst possible showcase for Pearson's own very considerable talents. Least forgivable is the destruction of the traceried gable, whose authenticity was obvious even without the corroboration of Dickinson's drawing.

The records of the original appearance of the front were assembled in Lethaby's two books on the Abbey, so it is possible to discuss the design almost as if the thirteenth-century fabric still existed. Like the rest of Henry III's church, the front approximates more closely to French than to English prototypes. As Lethaby noted, it owes most to

45

*Fig 8: Dummy portal, north transept front. Pen and wash drawing by Ambrose Poynter, 1818
(the British Architectural Library Drawings Collection).*

the west front of Amiens Cathedral, *c.* 1225-30. Admittedly, there are
no towers flanking the central section, but Amiens must be the source
of the open traceried gallery below the rose, of the motif of aisle windows behind the portals and of the way in which the fronts of the portals are made flush with those of the buttresses. (Hollar wrongly
shows the portals recessed).

Yet there is no question of Westminster's simply copying Amiens
or any other French façade. English preferences are most evident in
the design of the portals. Besides failing to attain the gargantuan scale
of the Amiens portals, they seem never to have sheltered statues
incorporated into the columns of the jambs. It is remarkable that with
such exceptionally strong French influence pervading everything
about Henry III's Westminster, the most fundamental innovation of
French Gothic sculpture was ignored in favour of the firmly
entrenched English usage of placing figures in niches. Clearly, Henry
of Reyns disapproved of the quasi-architectural function of the
French column figure, for throughout the Abbey major figure sculpture is always bounded by some kind of architectural 'frame'. The tympanum of the central portal is one of the most important illustrations

of this. It contained many small tracery-like compartments which must have limited the freedom of the figure sculptors far more than the friezes usual on French tympana.

English prejudices probably also account for the simple lancet windows between the portals and gallery, although there was a French precedent in the tall lancets of the Reims transept façades. The gallery rests on rather inelegant depressed pointed arches which, in order to clear the lancets, rise higher than the gallery floors inside. The internal structure of the church is more rationally reflected on the exterior by the rose, whose height equals that of the clearstorey. The tracery of the rose as preserved in the Dickinson drawing, and possibly also in the contemporary floor tiles of the chapter house (see p.114) was an extraordinarily up-to-date design for 1245, and were it not that the same is true of the tracery in the lower parts of both transepts, which were in hand before Henry of Reyns' death in 1253, one might be tempted to suggest that the rose tracery represents an up-dating of the original designs in the light of French developments of the late 1240s.

The square frame around the rose, the small circles in the spandrels and the core of sixteen radiating lancets each developing into two-light 'petals' all find their closest parallels in the north transept rose at Notre-Dame in Paris, which may have been begun a year or so after 1245. The only precedent for the glazing of the upper spandrels — technically the most daring detail — seems to be in Louis IX's chapel at St-Germain-en-Laye, begun c. 1238. A number of French roses which might have influenced Westminster are lost to us through having been replaced in the late Middle Ages. These include the west rose of the Sainte-Chapelle and the transept roses at Amiens. Interest in the tracery of Amiens is proved by the presence of oddly squashed-looking trefoils at the periphery of the rose and a similarly propor-tioned quatrefoil in the tympanum of the central portal, the former deriving from the Amiens nave triforium, the latter from the inner face of the north transept end wall.

The idea of using blind tracery on the tympana of portals seems to have originated on the west front of St-Nicaise in Reims, begun c. 1240. Whereas the tracery of the central tympanum at Westminster must have enclosed a series of figure groups, like its derivative on the Angel Choir at Lincoln, the side tympana almost certainly had tracery only. Poynter's drawing of 1818 (fig. 8) shows that the circles were then endowed, as they are now, with cinquefoil cusps that can never have left sufficient room for figure compositions. It is most unlikely that Dickinson put the cusps here as they are quite unlike those in the circles that decorated his now-destroyed central tympanum. His drawing shows no cusps, but then it also shows none in the lesser circles of the gable tracery, which are known from photographs and other records to have contained cusps.

The patterns of the tracery on all three tympana, as shown by Dickinson and corroborated by other pre-1719 sources, are of outstanding importance. The piled-up circles of the side tympana may have been suggested by the similarly arranged trefoils in the apse windows of the Sainte-Chapelle or by the quatrefoil-covered dado of the west portals at Amiens. However, the Westminster tympana take the idea of an infinitely extensible all-over pattern a stage beyond the French designs, for the complete circles are accompanied by segments of others seemingly cut off by the main enclosing arch. This design shares nothing except its basic elements with normal early thirteenth-century tracery types such as those in the body of the church. It anticipates by almost half a century the mesh-like 'reticulated' tracery which was pioneered in the east cloister at Westminster (see p.82) and thereafter became the most popular type of window tracery in early fourteenth-century England. The related pattern in the central tympanum is generated by piling up semi-circular arches. This can be seen as the first (by some seventy years) of the experiments that led up to the basic type of Perpendicular tracery apparently invented at Old St Paul's and quickly copied in the south and west cloisters at Westminster (see pp.83-4). The north gable tracery relates to that on the side tympana, though in this case there were French antecedents, the most important being the now-destroyed choir of Cambrai Cathedral, *c.* 1230-40.

Seen as a whole, the north front exemplifies the pivotal position of Westminster in the history of English Gothic: the early thirteenth-century French framework is made to carry an almost bewildering variety of themes, ranging from survivals of earlier English traditions, through borrowings from the latest Parisian work to anticipations of the Decorated Style, the most inventive and internationally important phase of English Gothic. That the details should occupy a higher imaginative plane than the large-scale architectural concepts is also prophetic of much English architecture of the next hundred years.

The North Side of the Nave

The five thirteenth-century bays of the nave continue the design of the eastern arm and transepts except that the triangular gallery windows now contain three circles and the circles in all windows are equipped with cinquefoil cusping. The saddlebacked terminations to the buttresses are an alteration of Blore's. It is curious that although the aisle and clearstorey tracery in the late medieval western bays is a thirteenth-century design, it is not a copy of that in the genuine thirteenth-century bays. The gallery windows, on the other hand, are quite careful imitations of those further east. The clearstorey of the fifth bay has unique tracery which may have been made purposely more like the eastern clearstorey because it completes a thirteenth-century bay. Alternatively, it may have been intended to effect a transition between the two designs which flank it. Or again, the intention may have been to use it throughout the western clearstorey bays. The door in the sixth bay led to the sacrist's offices, a large L-shaped building entered also from the north-west corner of the north transept. In the ninth to eleventh bays, the sculptured cornice of the triforium is original work of 1416-18.

The West Front

The west front succeeded the north transept front as the main public face of the Abbey once the towers had been completed in 1745. Comparison of the existing fabric with Hollar's engraving of 1655 shows the extent of Hawksmoor's alterations, reductions and completions of the unfinished Perpendicular front. The only important changes to the design were the simplification of the tracery of the main west window, the cladding of the lowest parts of the buttresses with shallow trefoil arches and the addition of a parapet to the west porch. The remarkable consistency of what was completed of the Perpendicular front suggests strongly that Henry Yeveley's designs were being followed with little or no modification down to the Reformation. In a sense this is a sequel to the late medieval architects' fidelity to the thirteenth-century nave design, although the stylistic gulf separating the mid-thirteenth century from the late fourteenth century is far greater than that between the latter period and the early sixteenth century. The basic concept of the two-tower west front no doubt conforms to thirteenth-century intentions, but its realization is wholly contemporary, apart from the windows lighting the west bays of the aisles and gallery.

After the north transept front, with its hesitant handling of the inherently cumbrous conventions of French façade design, the Perpendicular part of the west front registers as logical, disciplined and unified. The most unusual and impressive feature is the corner buttressing of the towers. These rise as sheer verticals allowing no reduction of mass in the ascent, an effect underscored by their being sheathed in post-like decorative buttresses enclosing Perpendicular tracery 'panels'. Monotony is avoided by varying the proportions of the panels and the weight of the horizontals.

Planted in front of the buttresses that flank the central section are

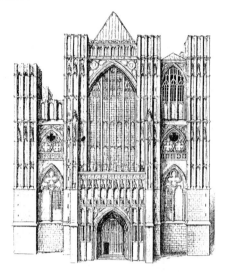

Fig 9: The west front. Etching by Wenceslaus Hollar from Dugdale's Monasticon Anglicanum, 1655.

narrow supplementary buttresses which help resist outward pressure from the high walls and vault of the nave and also serve to enclose the projecting west porch. This is of a distinctive southern English pattern in which a wide outer arch and smaller entrance are linked by a half-hexagonal space whose vault expands not only outwards but upwards. These aptly named 'welcoming porches' can be seen as combining the broad sloping jambs of the central portal of the north front at Westminster with the narrow vaults of the lateral portals. The immediate source is likely to have been the entrance in the choir screen of *c.* 1330 in Old St Paul's, which, like the Westminster west porch, was flanked by image niches. These and the now empty niches overhead contain attractively varied miniature vaults. They also illustrate the full development of that English tendency to compartmentalize figure sculpture which has already been discussed in relation to the north front. It is unclear whether the west porch is earlier or later than Yeveley's very similar porch on the north front of Westminster Hall, begun in 1394. The blind tracery on the sides of the porch includes a sort of 'tear drop' shape balanced on top of an oddly proportioned trefoil arch, all of which can be paralleled in the clearstorey of the nave at Canterbury Cathedral, probably again by Yeveley.

Hawksmoor completed the Perpendicular front up to the level of the main wall heads and above that installed a kind of entablature as a solid visual base for his own contribution. The panelling theme is continued, but with the emphasis on the isolation of each element rather than the overall effect. An arbitrary-looking sequence of horizontals marks the division between storeys and also, as one eventually realizes, the springing points of arched elements. The canopies over the real and dummy clock faces are actually not arches but segmental pediments, the most important of the few Classical elements spicing the design. Hawksmoor was attacked by Lord Burlington and others for this departure from the view expressed in Wren's letter of 1713 to the Dean that to make Classical additions to Gothic buildings 'would be to run into a Disagreeable Mixture which no Person of good Taste could relish'. The proportions of Hawksmoor's towers are also open to criticism. Whereas Yeveley had been at pains to give the towers sufficient bulk, Hawksmoor drew them inwards and so made them rather too slight in relation to the length and volume of the church. Their parapets echo that formerly on Henry VII's Chapel.

The South Side of the Nave
and the South Transept Front

To complete the tour of the exterior one must go into the cloister. The south side of the nave has a quite spectacular array of buttressing, necessitated by the presence of the north walk of the cloister. The buttress piers are omitted from the aisle and gallery wall, where they would have descended into and encumbered the north walk, and are set instead on the front wall of the walk. The walk is spanned by three tiers of flyers, the upper two continuing the regular flyers from the clearstorey, the lowest abutting the aisle vault. The clearstorey and aisle walls of the thirteenth-century bays are the only bays of the exterior endowed with the traditional English feature of blind lancets flanking each window. The cloister, for reasons discussed already, runs under the west aisle of the south transept. The regular windows on the west wall contrast oddly with the far more modern tracery of the cloister, for which see p. 81.

The south transept façade owes its anachronistically plate-traceried gable to Scott. His are the big conically capped turrets, which he claimed to have based on original fragments found in the masonry of the turrets he removed. In 1479-80 the pinnacles had been rebuilt and given ogee-profiled lead domes. The design of the rose of 1451-62, renewed last in 1901-2, must follow the original design fairly closely as it matches rather well Dickinson's drawing of the north rose. Below the rose are two-light windows but no gallery like that on the north transept. The simple buttresses are exactly like those which were on the north front until 1719. A plain and very deep round arch, possibly an addition, hides the lancet window in the south wall of the west aisle.

A TOUR OF THE INTERIOR

Westminster Abbey is famous for having taller internal proportions than any other major English medieval church. The actual height-width ratio in the central vessel is 3:1 as compared to 2.9:1 at Reims, 3.2:1 at Amiens and 3.4:1 at Beauvais. The internal height of 31.7m (104ft) is again exceptional in England — only the nave of York Minster is a near match — but it falls well short of the French High Gothic giants, for example the 35m (114ft) of Chartres, 43m (141ft) of Amiens and 47.5m (156ft) of Beauvais.

Plan of the abbey church and monastic offices

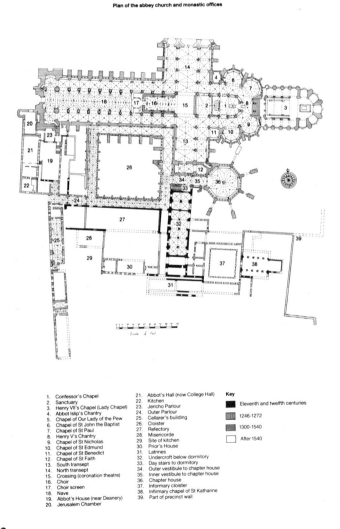

			Key
1. Confessor's Chapel	21. Abbot's Hall (now College Hall)		
2. Sanctuary	22. Kitchen		■ Eleventh and twelfth centuries
3. Henry VII's Chapel (Lady Chapel)	23. Jericho Parlour		
4. Abbot Islip's Chantry	24. Outer Parlour		▦ 1246-1272
5. Chapel of Our Lady of the Pew	25. Cellarer's building		
6. Chapel of St John the Baptist	26. Cloister		▩ 1300-1540
7. Chapel of St Paul	27. Refectory		
8. Henry V's Chantry	28. Misericorde		▢ After 1540
9. Chapel of St Nicholas	29. Site of kitchen		
10. Chapel of St Edmund	30. Prior's House		
11. Chapel of St Benedict	31. Latrines		
12. Chapel of St Faith	32. Undercroft below dormitory		
13. South transept	33. Day stairs to dormitory		
14. North transept	34. Outer vestibule to chapter house		
15. Crossing (coronation theatre)	35. Inner vestibule to chapter house		
16. Choir	36. Chapter house		
17. Choir screen	37. Infirmary cloister		
18. Nave	38. Infirmary chapel of St Katharine		
19. Abbot's House (near Deanery)	39. Part of precinct wall		
20. Jerusalem Chamber			

The central vessel of the eastern arm establishes the system applied throughout the rest of the building with only comparatively minor variations. The proportions of the main elevations are quite different from those of Reims in its final form, where the clearstorey is more dominant and the middle storey less so. Amiens is the obvious French precedent for Westminster's equating of the main arcade to the sum of the two upper storeys; and if Amiens was actually the model being followed here one may suspect that its attraction was the scope it gave for maintaining the English tradition of high middle storeys and relatively low clearstoreys. Nevertheless, the clearstorey must have been, to English eyes, one of the most striking things about Westminster. It was not only far taller than any earlier English clearstorey but far simpler in having no wall passage fronted by open arcades. From a French point of view it is odd that the openings occupy much less than the full width of the bays and so leave unarticulated strips of solid masonry next to the vault shafts. One possible explanation is that Henry of Reyns lacked the confidence to minimize the mass of the clearstorey wall and rely wholly on the flying buttresses to resist the enormous outward thrust of the high vaults. This seems unlikely because the area of contact between vaults and walls is kept as narrow as possible in order to transmit the thrust directly on to the flying buttresses. The narrowness of the vault-to-wall contact involves making the wall ribs stilted and twisting back the adjacent cells of the vault — the ideal context for clearstorey windows of maximum width.

So the fact that Westminster's clearstorey windows do not attain their potential width is more likely to reflect Henry of Reyns' aesthetic preferences than his want of technical skill. Two important early thirteenth-century French churches which he would have seen, Royaumont and St-Nicaise in Reims, exhibited this same combination of stilted wall ribs and relatively small clearstorey windows. Royaumont is the less likely source of the two, as the smallness of its windows reflected Cistercian puritanism rather than artistic conservatism. No such objection can be raised against St-Nicaise, a sumptuously finished Benedictine abbey church, whose influence can be detected elsewhere in Henry's design. Here again, an unusual model has been selected which reinforces Henry of Reyns' adherence to an English usage, for virtually all major early thirteenth-century churches on this side of the Channel have clearstorey windows considerably narrower than the bays to which they belong.

The gallery provides a further illustration of the same process, though in this case the balance is tipped more towards English tradi-

The north transept, showing vaulting in the west aisle and the upper parts of the east wall.

tion. Amiens Cathedral also has what is by French standards the rather elaborate scheme of twin tracery units, but there the subordination of middle storey to clearstorey is achieved by extending the shaft on the front of the central clearstorey mullion down between the tracery units. This concept of 'linkage' and the primacy it gives to the clearstorey are completely absent from Westminster, and, as in most important early thirteenth-century English churches, the middle storey is the single most eye-catching feature of the elevation. The scheme of paired units containing further subdivisions is also far more common in England than in France and is indeed the most widely used kind of middle storey in English Gothic before Westminster.

The tracery contained in each unit of the gallery is similar to that in the clearstorey, except that here, where there was evidently no concern to evoke the thirty-five-year-old design of Reims, the arches have the elegant trefoil cusps first used in window tracery at the Sainte-Chapelle. Nothing in England or France quite parallels the second layer of tracery set a few centimetres behind that facing the main vessel. The motif of superimposed layers of arcading appears in different guises in the wall arcades of Lincoln and Beverley and the triforia of mid-thirteenth-century French Rayonnant buildings like St-Denis or Tours, but the former are backed by solid masonry and the latter by glass. This use of double tracery against the shadowy spaces of a gallery is a calculated extravagance which lends the interior a subtly luxurious quality.

Perhaps the single most surprising thing in the elevations is the diapering, the carved trellis work of stylized flowers that covers the spandrels of the gallery and main arcades. Its impact must have been immeasurably heightened when it was enriched with the brilliant colours familiar from contemporary manuscript painting. The paint and gold disappeared long since in the periodic washings and brushings of the interior, but its presence is vouched for by the occasional areas of blank stone or marble which would have merged with the rest of the spandrels when coloured. Diaper originated in the embossed backgrounds to the figures on precious metal shrines such as that of the Three Kings at Cologne, and from here was taken up, along with other goldsmithing motifs, on the plinths of the west portals of Notre-Dame in Paris. It appeared in the same position at Amiens, but a more likely source is St-Nicaise in Reims, where it invaded very large areas of the west front. The only precedent for the use of diaper on the spandrels of major internal arches appears to be in the crossing tower built at Lincoln Cathedral from the late 1230s, although the diaper here is of a much simpler 'lattice' form, not specially reminiscent of goldsmiths' work. If Henry of Reyns and Henry III were aware of the origin of the French foliate diaper in sacred metalwork, its use at Westminster would provide a sequel to an otherwise unique aspect of the Sainte-Chapelle, its emulation of the colour and glitter of the shrine it housed. The presence of ersatz metalwork on the retable from the high altar (see p. 101) increases the chances that the environs of St Edward's shrine were quite consciously intended to echo the precious quality of its metalwork. Whatever its exact connotations may have been, the diapering is an unambiguous indication that

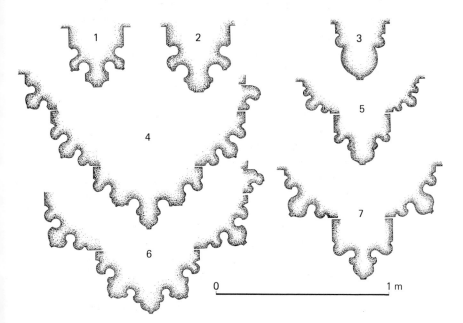

Fig 10: Thirteenth-century arch and rib profiles. (1) Diagonal rib of high vaults. (2) Transverse ribs of high vaults. (3) Diagonal ribs of vaults over ambulatory and aisles. (4) Main arcade arches of eastern arm and transepts. (5) Transverse arches of vaults over transept aisles. (6) Main arcade arches of eastern bays of nave. (7) Transverse arches of vaults over aisles of eastern bays of nave.

Henry III wished the Abbey to transcend ordinary levels of architectural enrichment.

Along with the tallness of the main spaces, it is the exceptionally high main arcades which contribute most to the exhilarating verticality of the interior. The Purbeck marble of the piers is a major concession to national Gothic traditions, and no doubt accounted for a major part of the materials bill. In fact the use of Purbeck at Westminster is quite profligate, for even such insignificant features as the roof slabs over passages are made of it. The piers rise 9.1m (30ft), cylinders of horizontally bedded Purbeck to which marble rings attach four slim shafts of the same stone bedded vertically. Once more this must be a case of the selection of an English design on the basis of its compatibility with the French overall scheme: superficially, the piers recall the horizontally bedded four-shaft piers at Reims and Amiens whereas the use of attached shafts and the detailing come much closer to some of the arcade piers at Salisbury Cathedral, begun in 1220. Even by French standards, the arches supported by the piers are extremely sharply pointed. Their undersides are ornamented with beautiful and complex mouldings (p. 56), an immensely costly form of embellishment more highly developed in England than anywhere else. Their inclusion in the elevations at Westminster is tantamount to a declaration that in this respect English Gothic was deemed superior to French.

The Westminster arcade mouldings do in fact incorporate several French profiles hitherto unknown in England, but their abundance and variety are wholly English. Structurally considered, the mouldings are a by-product of making the main walls much thicker than they would have been in France. Visually, they represent an exploration of the effects of layered depth permitted by the thickness. The English love of this fundamentally linear yet spatial form of decoration is most evident in the arcade arches but is not confined to them. The vigorously modelled frames around the clearstorey windows and the generously moulded and layered tracery of the gallery are further variations on the theme. In the outer orders of the gallery arches the tufts and blocks of foliage which usurp the regular mouldings bring an element of studied strangeness to this heavily opulent zone of the elevation.

The substitution of thick walls for the thin plate-like walls of French Gothic had other important consequences. The main arcade arches are nearly as thick as the piers they stand on, with the result that the shafts which receive the high vault have to be exceedingly slim if they are to rest on the capitals of the arcade piers. The shallow and plainly detailed arcade arches of Westminster's French counterparts leave much more of the piers available to support massive bundles of high vault shafts. The effect of this deviation from French practice is that when one looks along the length of the main vessels the vault shafts do not overpower the horizontals separating the storeys, as they do at, say, Chartres or Reims.

A complementary tempering of the verticality of French Gothic is achieved in the main apse where, for reasons set out on p. 40, the bays are not nearly so narrow and close-packed as in French apses. Here the piers can be given the same bulk and number of shafts as farther west, and the clearstorey can match that in the other bays, except that its windows fit snugly between the vault and its shafts. The gallery, on the other hand, has only a single two-light unit framed by substantial areas of plain walling. This rather casual relation of openings to bays also works against vertical emphasis. The clearstorey of the western bay is the most extreme illustration of this, for though the bay itself is almost one-and-a-half times the standard width, the window is no

The vault of the Chapel of St Nicholas.

wider than its fellows farther east. The western bay includes one other
oddity. The eastern halves of the arcade arches spring from the capital
with the same steep curvature as the arches to the east, before abruptly
changing pitch in order to arrive at the centre of the bay. Perhaps the
intention at this stage was that the western bay should be uniform with
the rest. Alternatively, the masons may have forgotten that the wider
span here demanded a slightly gentler curvature. In general, the
workmanship at Westminster is less exact than in contemporary
French churches or in some English churches, for example Beverley
or Wells.

   The high vault is a quadripartite rib vault whose cells are made of
blocks laid so as to meet at an angle at the ridges. This technique fell
from favour in France in the late twelfth century, around the same

time as it was becoming normal in England. The longitudinal ridge rib is in the same category of extreme rarity in France and commonness in England. It complements the features discussed above in stressing horizontality. The transverse and diagonal ribs have respectively wave and hollow chamfer mouldings (p. 56), inconspicuous harbingers of a later phase of English Gothic in which the deep hollows predominant in the Westminster mouldings give way to profiles that impart a weightier and less linear feel. The superb foliage bosses of the high vault have to compete with big rubbery leaves painted round them during Wren's restoration.

The Ambulatory and its Chapels

The plan of the ambulatory and its chapels is analysed on pp. 37-9. The spatial coherence of this part of the church was lost when Henry V's bridge-like chantry was inserted into the axial bay (see p. 129). The axial bay originally opened into the Lady Chapel, but when Henry VII's Chapel was built the severance of the two was completed by building a window wall over the reredos of Henry V's chantry. The thick arches dividing the vaults of the radiating chapels from those of the ambulatory are unmeaning remnants of the distinctive Reims system according to which every bay of vaulting is bounded by such arches. To have used heavy transverse arches in the ambulatory and aisles would have drawn attention to the irregular east bays of the aisles. The outer wall of each of these bays is so narrow that adjacent buttresses amalgamate into a mass of masonry which Henry rather despairingly fronted with a single blind lancet. (For the Chapel of Our Lady of the Pew built out later from the northern of these bays see p. 60). The second bays of the aisles are each flanked by an outer bay, a vestige of the two-bay double choir aisles of Reims. The thick transverse arches reappear in the outer aisles and from here continue throughout the transepts and nave. The windows here are also the pattern for the rest of Henry III's work. Their canted jambs and heads link the tracery and rear arches very effectively.

The idiosyncratic layout of the radiating chapels has been discussed on p. 39. Their windows are recessed far enough behind the wall plane to accommodate a wall passage. Reims was undoubtedly the source of this very rare feature, despite certain differences of detail. One of the differences is that it does not penetrate the sides of the chapels next to the ambulatory. The solid walls of these sides have blind tracery and serve as bases for the buttress piers receiving the flyers from the main apse. At Reims Jean d'Orbais had been able to void these walls by using a double range of buttresses. From the two eastern chapels the wall passages lead into the start of the passages in the side walls of the lost Lady Chapel. Presumably, these passages did not exist prior to the remodelling of the chapel in 1256. The trefoiled wall aracading in the radiating chapels must have been splendid before most of it was cut away for monuments. Sculptured spandrels in this position were unknown in France outside the Sainte-Chapelle and were quite rare in England. The radiating chapels at Reims have wall arcading but, like all the few French High Gothic examples, it is quite plain. Some of the chapels retain aumbries indicating that the altars faced more or less due east.

The north-west radiating chapel (St John the Baptist's) is entered through a lobby excavated out of the massive buttress north of the easternmost aisle bay. Originally the chapel of Our Lady of the Pew, this became a passageway c. 1524 when the building of Bishop Ruthall's tomb completed the severance of St John's Chapel from the ambulatory. There are three phases, all Perpendicular. The earliest and finest consists of the cusped entrance arch with angel busts carrying the arms of England and the Confessor, and the adjoining bay with tracery-sheathed walls and a tierceron vault whose central boss is carved with the Assumption. This work existed by 1376 when the chapel is mentioned as the setting of the anniversary masses celebrated for Aymer de Valence, whose tomb is on the opposite side of the aisle. The original half-doors gave a view of the image of Our Lady of the Pew donated by Aymer's widow and their ferocious spikes gave protection. Froissart says that in 1381 Richard II prayed here before his confrontation with Wat Tyler and the peasants at Blackheath, and it is likely that the wider north bay was added soon afterwards. In its tracerly-less walls are pieces of hooks for votive offerings. The painting on the north wall includes Richard's White Hart, on a spandrel of the niche now housing a modern alabaster image of Our Lady. The niche itself is of the first phase, and must therefore be re-set. The 1520s phase involved putting a door through the east side of the north bay, where the altar had been, and shearing off the north-east corner of this bay, which hitherto had jutted into St John's Chapel.

The Crossing and Transepts

The crossing of Westminster Abbey is not merely the intersection of the four arms of the church but the theatre in which coronations are staged. In the Middle Ages, the stage itself was a much loftier affair than in recent centuries. At Edward II's coronation it rose so high, an official memorandum says, that knights could have ridden under-

OPPOSITE: The transepts and crossing looking south.

The sanctuary from Henry III's 'royal box' (now the muniment room).

neath. As at Reims, there were two flights of steps, one between the choir stalls and the other before the high altar. The stage for Edward VI's coronation had twenty-nine steps on each side and seven more under the throne. Apart from its obvious symbolic value, the height would be needed in order to make the king visible above the screens continuing the line of the choir stalls, always assuming these were not temporarily removed. Elevated some 8m (25ft) above the pavement, the crowned king would have been enabled to receive the shouted acclamation of his subjects not only from the floor of the transepts but also, perhaps, from the galleries. The galleries have certainly been used in this way in recent coronations though it is unclear how far back the custom goes. If these spaces did originally fulfil a ceremonial function, their size and careful internal finish would be only what was appropriate. Perhaps the acclamation at Henry III's own coronation had been shouted from the galleries of the Confessor's church. It is unlikely that such a usage could have derived from Reims, where there are no galleries, only shallow triforia.

To allow room for the coronation stage the crossing piers do not project as much as in most churches intended to be crowned by a central tower. Above the springings of the crossing arches are heads carrying bases for the shafts of the unbuilt lantern vault. Hawksmoor's big relieving arches and low single lancets show surprisingly little sense of occasion. The lath and composition crossing vault of 1803 was bombed in 1941 and succeeded by a wooden ceiling painted to look like a gargantuan Minton tile. As Wren noted in 1713, the crossing piers bend inwards in response to thrusts from the main arcades in all four arms. To arrest this distortion he reinstated the iron ties between the arcade capitals, the originals of which had been, he said 'stolen away'. There were iron or timber ties in many French Gothic churches, and in the choir of Canterbury built by the Frenchman, William of Sens, but these were all removed at the completion of work. So was Wren reinstating a lost feature of the thirteenth-century design when he put back these aesthetically dubious ties? Seventeenth-century engravings show one or two still in place, and the chances are that the timber ties in the ambulatory are original. Further evidence favouring Wren is the survival into the nineteenth-century of a full set of ties in the Salisbury chapter house, a near-copy of that at Westminster.

The transepts show Henry of Reyns' design to great advantage, without the liturgical divisions and discrepant bay widths of the eastern arm. The length of the transepts makes them relatively autonomous and not, as in most French cathedrals, mere annexes to the main east-west vessel. Four bays is a common number for the transepts of major early thirteenth-century English churches. Whereas the bays to east and west of the crossing are wider than normal, the adjoining transept bays are narrow — a dilution of the Reims concept of a coronation theatre of maximum spaciousness with wide bays on all four sides of the crossing. Where the west aisle of the south transept ought to be there is the east walk of the cloister surmounted by what functioned as Henry III's 'royal box'. Access was by a spiral stair at the south-east corner of the transept and by passages through the south wall. In front of the south window of the royal box is a lobby with three lancets and three rib vaults, as in the windows at the ends of the north transept aisles. The figure sculpture here is particularly fine, as befitted its visibility from close quarters by the King. The solid wall

63

below this room incorporates dummy piers, that at the corner of the cloister with extra shafts. The two tiers of blind lancets no doubt framed paintings before they were commandeered for monuments. Round the corner is the east processional door topped by three startlingly large blind quatrefoils in circles.

Tiered lancets, blind open and glazed, occupy the arcade level of the south wall. The blocked arch towards the west corner led from the monks' dormitory into a projecting spiral night stair destroyed in the early eighteenth century. The windows at gallery level are enriched versions of the regular gallery openings. The inspiration for decorating the spandrels with life-size figures (see p. 90) may have been the Sainte-Chapelle where smaller reliefs of angels occupy the spandrels of the wall arcade and statues of apostles stand between the windows. On the other hand, St Hugh's Choir at Lincoln, begun 1192, has busts in the spandrels of the wall arcade. French transept end walls are usually very plain, but the south wall at Westminster displays an impressive and carefully modulated transition from the darkest and most solid level at the base to the brilliance and openness of the great rose. At the level of the rose the front plane of the wall is omitted altogether, its notional position indicated by the shallow gap between the vaults and the rose. This gap has a flat ceiling which enables the upper spandrels of the rose to be glazed. At the foot of the south wall is the door to St Faith's Chapel (for which see below, p. 65).

In the east aisle of the south transept, the south window is another of the innovatory designs used whenever imitation of the Reims tracery was not the paramount consideration. It is an example of the so-called 'Y-tracery', in which the subdivisions have the same curvature as the enclosing arch. The idea could have come from the internal tympanum of the north transept portal at Amiens or from the western nave chapels at Lincoln. Its appearance here is admittedly fairly inconspicuous but not so much so as to prevent one from seeing it as the beginning of the widespread late thirteenth-century vogue for Y-tracery. In the adjoining part of the east wall is the king's entrance from the palace. The nearby door to the 'royal box' also leads to the chapter house undercroft, almost certainly built as a strongroom for the regalia. The east window of this bay and the corresponding windows in the other bays at the transept corners are wider than their neighbours. The windows of the west corner bays at Reims were also exceptionally wide, until they were reduced, presumably some time after Henry of Reyns' visit; but whereas the Reims windows reflected the extra width of the tower-supporting bays to which they belonged, at Westminster the corner bays are of regular width and do not carry towers. So the extra width of these windows, which is gained by omitting the canting from one jamb, has to be classed, along with the thick transverse arches of the aisle vaults, as an element copied from Reims without any concern for its original significance there.

In most respects, the north transept balances the southern arm. The end wall here is less impressive partly because of Pearson's hideous rose but also because of the lack of glazing behind the gallery-level openings. Glazing was impossible here as the external gallery on the north front had four tracery units instead of three, as well as a higher floor level. Unlike the east aisle, the west aisle housed no altars and was accessible through its own portal in the north front.

St Faith's Chapel, off the south transept, occupies the space left over between the chapter house, its vestibule and the end wall of the transept. It is a high plain room vaulted in three compartments, of which the easternmost is sexpartite, a strangely old-fashioned choice. At the west end is a gallery linking the monks' dormitory to the night stair. The recess underneath was probably used for storage. The only lighting is borrowed from the chapter house vestibule.

The Order of Construction of the Eastern Parts

Some clues to the sequence in which the east end and transepts were built are yielded by small variations in detailing. One such is the size of the diapering over the main arcades. In the two western bays of the eastern arm, the north arcade spandrels were begun with the small diaper used in the rest of this vessel and on the east side of the south transept, and they were finished with the large diaper used in the rest of the transepts and the nave. This evidence that the south transept was well advanced on its east side even before the eastern arm was finished not only confirms the general east-west sequence of work, which one would assume anyway, but proves that priority was given to the transept on whose completion the efficient functioning of the monastic offices depended.

Complementary indications of this sequence are provided by the incidence of a strange conical element which occurs at the springing of the aisle-level vaults and main arcade arches. The outer walls of the eastern arm and the east and south walls of the south transept lack this feature and may therefore be designated the first walls to be built, not necessarily in a separate campaign. Conical springings come into use increasingly towards the west end of the eastern arm and appear consistently in the outer wall of the north transept and on the piers of the east arcade of the south transept. After this they fall out of use again. The building accounts show that John of Gloucester took over while the east cloister walk was in building but before the 'royal box' above it had been begun. Since this side of the south transept omits conical springings and uses large diaper, it seems clear that John also built the similarly detailed high walls of the north transept between 1253 and 1259, the year in which demolition of the Confessor's nave began. The conical springings plot the later parts of Henry of Reyns' work. Henry's willingness to change his mind as work progressed is also evident from the pier bases. The six piers of the apse and the corresponding shafts in the ambulatory all have polygonal sub-bases. One might argue that these were demarcators of the specially sacred area round the Confessors' shrine, although this would be to presuppose an impressively attentive architectural public. A mere change of mind must account for the lack of a symmetrical pattern in the succession of 'waterholding' bases by bases with triple rolls.

When work reached the east end of the nave, John of Gloucester took the opportunity to revise the original designs. There was no question of any radical departures, but John evidently had his own views on what was best for the longest arm of the church. In order to buttress the west side of the crossing some parts of the nave had to be in position prior to the 1259 order for the demolition of the old nave and the start of the replacement. What these parts were is fairly clear as further but less important revisions occur in the first bay of the clearstorey and the second bay of the gallery and arcade. These last changes must be due to Robert of Beverley who succeeded John in 1260, when little more than demolition can have been carried out under the 1259 order. The easternmost springers of the high vault appear to be integral with the west crossing arch, so the decision to switch from simple quadripartite to tierceron vaulting must be John's. This luxuriant and distinctively English type of vault had been pioneered in the Lincoln nave (begun *c.* 1220) and the Ely presbytery (1234-50).

The east jambs of the easternmost clearstorey windows are of the type used by Henry of Reyns, but the rest are of the canted type hitherto confined to the aisles. The gallery also starts off uniform with the original designs, but in the second bay Robert omits all foliage carving except the diaper. Like his high vault, John's arcade elaborates the original concept. The piers have eight shafts instead of four and those at the cardinal points are now integral with the core rather than attached to it. The arch mouldings are also revised, though less obviously. Robert follows this design except that he links the central pier shafts to the high vault responds and substitutes bronze for marble shaft-rings. The latter change also occurs in the aisle responds. John alters the relation of the aisle vault ribs to the piers, and then, over the second pier, Robert changes it back to something very like that in the transept aisles. Robert's vault infilling differs slightly from

John's, and at the first opportunity, in the third bay, he switches to thinner diagonal ribs. Robert gives the circles of the aisle windows five flat-ended cusps like those in his triforium tracery.

More conspicuous than these subtleties is the introduction into the nave spandrels, almost certainly by John, of heraldic shields hung by their straps from human heads. It has been suggested that this motif imitates the real shields hung as wall decoration in the hall of the Paris Temple, where Henry III and Louis IX dined in 1254. Robert of Beverley's work stops one bay west of the choir screen. His last pier on the north side has base mouldings slightly different from the rest.

Colour in Henry III's Church

The contribution of colour to the thirteenth-century architecture has to be visualized mainly from the recollections of nineteenth- and twentieth-century architects, including Lethaby, for virtually no paint survives now other than on the shields in the nave aisles and the sculptures below the rose windows in the transepts. As has been mentioned already, Westminster and the Sainte-Chapelle were exceptions to the general Gothic trend towards near-monochrome masonry. Admittedly, some of the plain walling here did receive the standard treatment of whitewash and imitation masonry joints lined out in red, but much larger areas were fully polychromed. The metalwork-inspired diapering on the triforium and arcade spandrels was gilt on a red ground and must have created a scintillating contrast to the glossy grey-brown Purbeck of the piers and shafts. On all arch and rib mouldings projecting parts were gilt and hollows were red, blue or green. In the south transept, according to one observer, the main arcades had alternate lengths of dark and light colouring spotted like marble. In the clearstorey, the brilliant, mostly primary colours of the stained glass would have been offset by white lined out walls. Around the bosses of the high vault were coloured and gilt foliage sprays, probably rather like those still preserved at Salisbury, where the cells of the vault are lined out on white. The greatest concentration of colour, as of sculpture, was on the wall arcading in the chapels and aisles. Lethaby surmised that the aisle-level windows were greyish-green grisaille glass with only small areas of bright colour. It seems more likely that most were completely coloured and made up of narrative medallions such as survive in Jerusalem Chamber and the library. Grisaille survived until the late nineteenth century in one of the southern radiating chapels, probably in the less prominent windows.

The north wall of the nave, showing the junction between Henry III's work (right) and the late medieval continuation (left).

The oldest parts of the fourteenth-century nave continuation are the aisle walls designed by John Palterton in 1376. By comparison with the thirteenth-century work, the general impression is leaner and more energetic. The mouldings are shallower and the arch curvatures subtler. The major changes are the omission of wall passages and marble shafts, the latter possibly in response to Cardinal Langham's urgings that work should not be delayed for the sake of using marble. How far west Palterton's work extends is not certain, but it may be that Yeveley's advent is marked by the omission of the foliage spandrels from the wall arcade in the western bays. The tower bays include narrow supplementary compartments, to give extra width to the west front. The west windows are kept centred by the ingenious expedient of glazing only the inner of the two lancets. In the penultimate bay of the south aisle is an early sixteenth-century wooden oratory connecting with the private quarters of the abbot's house.

The reversion to marble for the piers coincided with Yeveley's takeover of the nave works in 1387, even if it was not his decision. The pier bases differ slightly from Palterton's. The only major revisions to the thirteenth-century main elevations are the omission of diaper and marble vault shafts. The possible explanations for the unique clearstorey design in the fifth bay have been discussed on p. 49. The vault of this bay is stiff with Tudor badges and includes a wheel for Catharine of Aragon. The eminently un-French longitudinal sweep of the nave vault is interrupted only by the arch between the western towers. The Perpendicular style appears untrammelled only on the west wall. The window of eight lights and four transoms (simplified by Hawksmoor) is linked to panelling round the west door and set in a canted frame overlaid with closer panelling. Among the finishing touches made to the nave in 1507-9 was the washing down of its walls, doubtless stained by the weather before the roof was built. There is no record of painting, so it appears that in the end the nave looked very different from the thirteenth-century work, despite its conformity in strictly architectural matters.

Chapter Three

HENRY VII'S CHAPEL

IF HENRY VII's plans had ever been completely fulfilled, his chapel might today bear the name of Henry VI. The hope was that the last Lancastrian king would be canonized and that his shrine would stand beside the tomb of the first Tudor, conferring on the new line both spiritual lustre and dynastic legitimacy. In 1494 it was intended that the two Henrys would lie in a new chapel on the site of Henry III's Chapel of St Edward in Windsor Castle, but in 1498 Henry VII accepted the Westminster monks' claim that Henry VI had planned to be buried near the Confessor's shrine, and Windsor was abandoned in favour of the Lady Chapel at Westminster. In anticipation of the canonization and the transferral of Henry VI's body, the thirteenth-century chapel was demolished and replaced by what almost amounted to a second church. In the event, however, the canonization process languished, Henry VI's bones remained at Windsor and Henry VII's monument was set up behind the main altar, where a shrine would normally have been. The foundation stone was laid on 24 January 1503 and the structure was apparently close to completion when the King died on 21 April 1509. At this point, expenditure totalled £14,856, and eight days before his death Henry made over a further £5,000 to complete the building. Decoration and furnishing probably continued until 1512. Unfortunately, the building accounts are lost, and with them the certain identification of the architect. There can be little doubt that he was one of the three 'king's master masons' who made estimates for Henry VII's tomb in 1506, namely Robert Vertue, Robert Janyns and John Lebons. Janyns is the strongest candidate, as the exterior of the chapel owes its most distinctive features to his main documented work, Henry VII's Tower at Windsor, begun before 1499, and other elements of the design, notably the main interior elevations, are closely modelled on St George's Chapel,

Henry VII's Chapel from the north-east.

Windsor, begun in 1475 to the designs of Janyns' father, Henry, and probably continued by the son between *c.* 1495 and 1506. Robert Vertue's rebuilding of Bath Abbey, begun in 1501, shows no points of close resemblance to Henry VII's Chapel. No buildings by John Lebons before 1503 are known, and nothing in his later work at Hampton Court and Christ Church, Oxford suggests that he was the designer of Henry VII's Chapel.

THE EXTERIOR

The chapel consists of a clearstoreyed central vessel of four bays, side aisles and an apse with five radiating chapels. The similarity to the east end of the main church and the exact match between the dimensions of the main vessels of chapel and eastern arm show that Westminster's second royal saint was to be accorded honours equalling those of the first. There is nothing backward-looking about the artistic means used to achieve this parity, for the exterior treatment ranks as one of the most original designs in all Gothic architecture. On the aisles and chapels conventional traceried windows are abandoned in favour of bay windows of complex, broken plan, and the bays are separated by buttresses transformed into polygonal turrets. All this is welded into one striated crystalline mass by the application of the densest possible grid of Perpendicular panelling. Variety is achieved by making the aisles wider than the chapels and by differentiating their windows: bows sandwiched between half-bows on the aisles; canted bays with a central bastion-like projection on the chapels. Bows, bays, bastions and turrets are of course primarily secular motifs, and Henry VII's Chapel is exceptional among major Gothic churches in being so indebted to palatial architecture.

The immediate source of both the fanciful bays and the onion-domed turrets must have been Henry VII's Tower at Windsor and the river front of the destroyed palace at Richmond (1498-1501), although simpler ogee-profiled domelets had already made one of their earliest English appearances on the south transept of the Abbey in 1479-80. All these domes were of lead, as were those on the western stair turrets of Henry VII's Chapel until 1809. Those on the buttress-turrets are amongst the earliest stone examples in northern Europe. The ultimate ancestry of this exotic motif must include the representations of Jerusalem in early fifteenth-century Netherlandish paintings and in the canopies of Brussels-made wooden altarpieces of the 1470s and 1480s. The strength of the influence from indigenous palace architecture is unmistakably a sign of changing patterns in patronage, but the fact that the bays and turrets of the chapel outdid those of the most ambitious English secular buildings of c. 1500 exemplifies the continuing pre-eminence of church building almost on the eve of the Reformation.

Interrupting the upper panels on the buttress-turrets and encrusting the cornice at the base of the parapet are carved badges proclaiming Henry VII's links with the Lancastrian and Yorkist dynasties. Together with the Tudor roses commemorating his marriage to Edward IV's eldest daughter, there are portcullises for his mother, Margaret Beaufort, great-granddaughter of Edward III, and fleurs-de-lys for his grandmother, Catherine of Valois, widow of Henry V. On the 'pinnacles' panelling gives way to niches which until the early eighteenth century were populated by statues of Apostles and Old Testament figures. The onion domes have fictive shingles, and at the

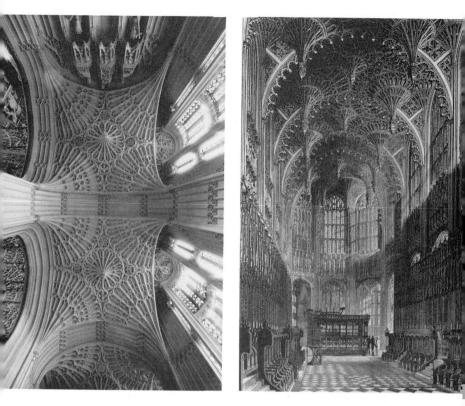

LEFT: The vault over the south aisle of Henry VII's Chapel. RIGHT: The interior of Henry VII's Chapel, looking south-east. Aquatint from Ackermann's Westminster Abbey, 1812.

time of writing some have received gyrating gilded weathervanes replacing those lost in the eighteenth century.

Compared to the lower walls, the clearstorey is conventional, its big windows worked into a continuum of panelling less consistent than that below. The parapet and pinnacles are the only unauthenticated details of the extremely careful refacing done in 1809-22, under James and Benjamin Wyatt. Judging from Hollar's engraving of 1654, the original parapet was similar to that on the chapel at Windsor which Henry VII first intended as his and Henry VI's burial place. The buttress 'pinnacles' and the flyers are the most entertaining features of the upper storey. The flyers are pierced by circles filled with varied tracery, and on the upper tier are what a second glance reveals to be not crockets but downward-scrambling files of beasts.

73

THE INTERIOR

The Vestibule and Aisles

Access to the main chapel is by a vestibule on the site of the west end of the thirteenth-century Lady Chapel. This arrangement allows the body of the chapel to expand to the same width as the main vessel of the eastern arm, and the twelve steps it contains enable the floor level to be the same as in the Confessor's chapel. At the west end is a triple entrance built on to the three arches at the east side of Henry V's chantry and echoed by the entrance into the chapel proper. Between the arches are heraldic beasts on octagonal pillars, a favourite adjunct of early Tudor palace buildings and gardens. In any other context, this elegant and sumptuously detailed room would be an attraction in itself. The vault is a four-centred tunnel overlaid with a close mesh of tracery panels and studded, like much of the chapel beyond, with roses, portcullises and fleurs-de-lys.

The side aisles have to be entered from the vestibule as the stalls divide them off completely from the main vessel. The vaults are fan vaults of square plan, the easiest kind to build since the upper limits of the conoids can start and finish at the centres of the sides. In the centre of each component is a pendant supported independently of the conoids by being made the keystone of heavy diagonal 'ribs' concealed above the conoids. In Robert Vertue's aisle vaults at Bath Abbey the pendants are carried by quite different means. Much the most spectacular feature of the aisles is the way the window walls ripple along the outer edges of the fans without touching them. The windows are curtains of glass rising to stellate ribbed ceilings set some way above the crowns of the vaults. The unsupported outer edges of the fans lend them an insubstantial awning-like quality which is complemented by the flatness of the panelled transverse arches. There are earlier examples of such transverse arches used in fan vaulted side aisles, notably at St George's, Windsor, but here they solve the unique problem of how to incorporate the broad backs of the buttress-turrets into the interior elevations. At the west end of each aisle a tiny fan vaulted lobby is contrived below the light well for the window. The images in the reredoses and the angel friezes below them are the only figural adjuncts to these virtuoso ensembles.

The Main Chapel

Until the choir stalls were extended eastwards in *c.* 1810, the east bays of the aisles were divided from the central vessel by stone screens of triple-bow shape echoing the aisle windows. The lower parts of identical screens remain in front of the two western radiating chapels, but the chapels further east were unscreened. All five radiating chapels are in effect deep recesses, for there is no ambulatory linking them. Their dividing walls are wedge-shaped in plan, their inner edges treated as responds matching those on the freestanding piers in the body of the chapel. The walls between the western radiating chapels and the aisles are thick rectangular masses whose inner faces are made to support a broad and richly decorated arch marking the western limit of the apse. The axial chapel shows no sign of having housed an altar, and it is safe to assume that this was designated as the site of Henry VI's shrine, whose altar would have been attached to its western face. The niche in the most honourable place, the centre of the north wall, must have contained an image of Henry VI as its pedestal is carved with the initials H R. Opposite, on the south wall, is St Peter, the main patron of the Abbey, flanked by the two successfully canonized royals, St Edward and St Edmund.

The main elevations are rather closely modelled on those of St George's, Windsor, but so consistently enriched that there can be no doubt of the intention to outstrip that greatest architectural achievement of the Yorkist kings. The window which almost fills the west wall combines the most imposing features of the east window of the main chapel at Windsor (now altered) and the west window of the adjoining chapel where Henry VII's tomb was originally to have stood. In the lateral elevations the borrowings from St George's range from decorative details like the angel frieze above the arcade, to such fundamentals as the bold uprights shared by the high vault and the clearstorey rear arches, and the main arcades which are shallow towards the central vessel though deeply moulded to the aisles. Shallow arcades and boldly projecting shafts were among the aspects of French Gothic rejected by Henry of Reyns but taken up about a century later by the earliest exponents of Perpendicular architecture. In southern England at least, they remained essential parts of the style. Enrichments of the St George's scheme include the five-light clearstorey windows in place of four-lighters, the tracery in the main arcade spandrels, the panels flanking the vault shafts and, above all, the inclusion of a 'triforium' formed of a band of enriched images. The only English precedent for such a use of figure sculpture is in the choir of Wells Cathedral, of c. 1330-40. Despite such phenomenal enrichment, the main lines of the design remain as clear and 'readable' as at Windsor, or rather they would do so if it were not for the banners of the Knights of the Bath which now hang over the stalls. These banners are an almost insurmountable obstacle to appreciation of the chapel as a whole, for in obscuring the walls they also obscure the studied contrast between the coolly rectilinear elevations and the

The vault of Henry VII's Chapel.

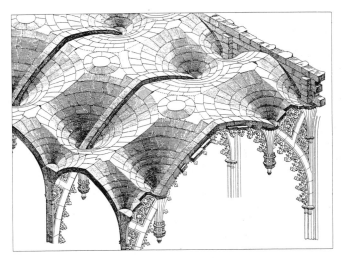

Fig 11: The constructional technique of the vault of Henry VII's Chapel.
Engraving after drawing by Robert Willis from Transactions of the Royal Institute
of British Architects, I (1842).

dazzling pyrotechnics overhead.

The vault is the climax not only of Henry VII's Chapel but of the whole development of English late medieval vault design. In every way it is the most perfect existing example of a pendant fan vault, the most ambitious kind of vaulting current in the Perpendicular period. It is in fact the only large-scale fan vault built wholly in the distinctive technique of jointed masonry shells (Fig. 11) and without recourse to the traditional rib-and-panel method. Small-scale pendant fan vaults had existed in England for a long time, for instance in the Founder's Chapel at Tewkesbury *c.* 1380 and the oratory next to the Beauchamp Chapel at Warwick *c.* 1441-9, but all the few pendant vaults on a large scale which predate Henry VII's chapel are rib vaults, for example those in the Lady Chapel at Christchurch Priory *c.* 1405 and the Divinity School at Oxford *c.* 1478-88.

The Christchurch and Oxford vaults furnish partial precedents for the other major ingredient of the Westminster vaults, the transverse arches on to which the fans are threaded, so to speak. Oxford parallels the use of openwork tracery between the outer parts of the vault and the transverse arches, and also the device of incorporating the main stones of the pendants into the transverse arches. But whereas at Oxford the transverse arches are fully visible, in the Christchurch and Westminster vaults they disappear above the cells of the central part. At Westminster the vanishing act is not quite complete, as the cusping on the undersides of the arches is allowed to extend across the full width of the chapel. Pendant cusping is very rare in England, and the most likely source of the motif is the fan vault of 1488 over Bishop Alcock's Chantry at Ely. This was designed by someone very familar with St George's, Windsor, possibly the original architect, Henry Janyns.

Although the ground for the Westminster vault was well prepared in the sense that practically every element of its design had been used before, nothing can detract from the marvellous skill with which these elements are deployed. No other late medieval English vault on this scale is a shell only 9cm (4in) thick between the tracery 'ribs', and no earlier fan vault over rectangular bays had replaced the flat centre of each compartment with a pendant. The artistry at whose disposal this technical virtuosity is placed can be illustrated only with a few examples. By using pendant cusping to mark the position of the invisible central parts of the transverse arches, a fine balance is struck between preserving continuity with the strong bay divisions in the outer parts of the vault and the need to avoid constraining the splendid wheeling effect of the pendant fans. The broad arch between the rectangular bays and the apse, already explained as a continuation of the solid walls dividing aisles from radiating chapels, serves also the purely aesthetic function of playing down the slight but necessary disparity between the diameters of the lowest horizontal ribs in the two parts of the vault. The carousel effect of the six closely spaced pendants in the apse contrasts markedly with the pillarless hall-church effect of the rest, but the whole is given unity by the simple and apparently unique device of recessing the panels so much that they become little more than shadows emphasizing the filigree of the surface tracery. It is this spider's web weightlessness which stays longest in the mind's eye and earns the vault its place among the most captivating creations of medieval architecture.

Chapter Four

THE PRECINCTS

IT IS ALMOST IMPOSSIBLE to visualize how the Abbey looked when it was still encircled by a high precinct wall pierced only by four gates. A sense of enclosure persists to the south of the abbey church, but the churchyard to the north is reduced to a strip of lawn and trees, while on the east and west there is nothing at all to muffle the roar of traffic.

It would, however, be wrong to picture the medieval churchyard as an oasis of calm, for by the fourteenth century, if not earlier, it had become a valuable piece of real estate lined with houses and commercial premises, among them the house near the Lady Chapel where William Caxton was to set up the first English printing press in 1476. By the early sixteenth century the churchyard was known as the sanctuary, on account of the abbey's privilege of sanctuary and the houses there for the sanctuary men. Apart from the parish church of St Margaret's, the most important building in the churchyard was the free-standing belfry, built in 1249-53 for the prodigious set of bells donated by Henry III and demolished in 1750. This was a squat and severely plain structure with sides 23m (75ft) long, surmounted by a bell-stage and spire of lead-clad timber. The angle of the north transept and nave was taken up with the two-storey sacrist's offices.

The other large open area within the precincts, Dean's Yard (called 'the Elms' in the Middle Ages) has also changed out of all recognition, though it retains its most substantial medieval buildings, the cellarer's range and abbot's house. This was the outer court of the monastic offices, given over to working buildings such as the granary (later the dormitory of Westminster School), bakehouse, brewhouse and barn.

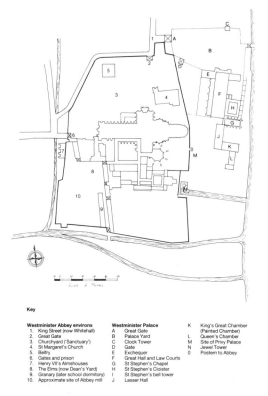

THE ENVIRONS OF WESTMINSTER ABBEY AS IN C. 1540

Key

Westminster Abbey environs		Westminster Palace			
1.	King Street (now Whitehall)	A	Great Gate	K	King's Great Chamber
2.	Great Gate	B	Palace Yard		(Painted Chamber)
3.	Churchyard ('Sanctuary')	C	Clock Tower	L	Queen's Chamber
4.	St Margaret's Church	D	Gate	M	Site of Privy Palace
5.	Belfry	E	Exchequer	N	Jewel Tower
6.	Gates and prison	F	Great Hall and Law Courts	0	Postern to Abbey
7.	Henry VII's Almshouses	G	St Stephen's Chapel		
8.	The Elms (now Dean's Yard)	H	St Stephen's Cloister		
9.	Granary (later school dormitory)	I	St Stephen's bell tower		
10.	Approximate site of Abbey mill	J	Lesser Hall		

The parts of the medieval precinct wall surviving here and in Abingdon Street may contain early thirteenth-century work, but the stretch around the Jewel Tower was certainly built *c.* 1374-6, once Edward III's seizure of abbey land for the tower was seen to be a *fait accompli*. The only buildings of the precinct discussed in detail in this chapter are those accessible to the public. The plans above and on p. 52 show the relation of these to the precinct as a whole.

THE CLOISTER

The Thirteenth-Century Work

Henry of Reyns began the north bays of the eastern walk of the cloister in 1253. The tracery is a variation on the theme of piled up forms discussed in relation to the north transept portals: three unencircled trefoils over three lights. Throughout the cloister, only the heads of the windows have ever been glazed; below the springing

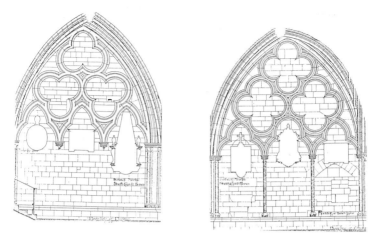

LEFT: Fig 12: Thirteenth-century blind tracery in the east walk of the cloister and RIGHT: Fig 13: The north walk. Drawing by T. MacLaren, 'The Building News', February 15 1884.

were wooden shutters attached by iron fittings. The windows are echoed in blind tracery on the back walls. On the east side of the corner bay, mullions are omitted to leave room for presses housing the books used for study in the north walk.

Henry of Reyns' work includes the east processional door, whose most distinctive features are its French crocket capitals and the continuous bands of diaper on the inner order. The third bay of the east walk is darkened by the stair turret at the south-west corner of the transept and divided from the bays to the north by a broad arch marking the position of the south wall of the transept. South of the chapter house entrance is the door of the day stair to the dormitory (now leading to the library), with a two-light tracery tympanum. The Romanesque wall of the dormitory undercroft begins here, on a different alignment from the thirteenth-century work.

The blind tracery in the north walk differs from that in the east walk in having three quatrefoils rather than trefoils and also more delicate mouldings. These changes are probably due to John of Gloucester. The window space of the easternmost bay is blocked by one of the deep buttresses to the west wall of the transept, but whereas the unlit bay in the east walk is undecorated, this has blind tracery matching that on the north wall. In the windows of the north walk circles replace quatrefoils, a change attributable to Robert of Beverley. The new pattern can be seen as a simplification of the blind tracery on the north transept gable. The cusping, made of separate stones, was restored by Scott. The two west bays date from the 1370s, like the nave aisle wall of which they are part, though the imitation of the thirteenth-century design is even closer than in the nave. The only things that betray the date are the profile of the bases and the structural continuity with the avowedly Perpendicular north-west corner bay. That the back wall was intended by Robert of Beverley to have blind tracery, as in the other bays, is proved by the cut away springing at the eastern edge of the eastern bay.

The Early Fourteenth-Century Work

Concern for overall unity was not allowed to inhibit invention in the southern half of the east walk. Admittedly, the base and capital mouldings on the window wall are quite closely matched to those already installed on the back wall, but the windows themselves exhibit the inventiveness and finesse of Decorated architecture at its best. The date of c. 1344-9 usually applied to these bays is at odds with their stylistic character, which suggests a date c. 1300-10. Confirmation that they are as early as this is provided by Scott's testimony that the west window of the chapter house had been replaced in the same style, an alteration which must have been necessitated by the burning of the roofs of the dormitory and chapter house vestibule in the 1298 fire. It is inconceivable that the chapter house should have had to wait over forty years for a new west window. Furthermore, the east cloister walk was the most important walk both ceremonially and functionally and hence the most likely to be given priority in the post-fire rebuilding.

The dating of this part of the cloister is of some moment, for if it belongs to the 1340s it is extremely old-fashioned, but if it is of c. 1300-10 it is among the most advanced works of its time. All windows save one have ogee reticulated tracery, the simplest and, eventually, the commonest form of the curvilinear tracery pioneered in England around 1300. It would be highly appropriate if these were the first examples, for the nearest approximation to this tracery in thirteenth-century architecture is that on the tympana of the north transept portals. To turn the transept pattern into the cloister pattern one has only to omit the upper and lower sixths of the tangential circles. The all-over quality of reticulated tracery is particularly useful in the east cloister as it obviates individual adjustment to fit the differing heights and widths of the window heads.

The bay containing the chapter house entrance has a specially beautiful and complex design. It is reticulation, but based on a grid of diamonds. The sides of each diamond are undulating lines and the

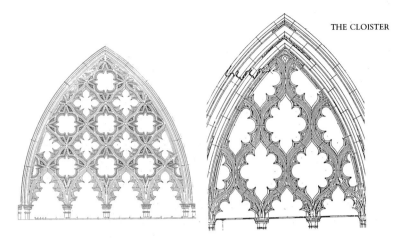

Fourteenth-century blind tracery in the east walk of the cloister. LEFT: Fig 14: Window opposite the Chapter House entrance, from William Caveller's Select Specimens of Gothic Architecture, 1839. RIGHT: Fig 15: Window south of previous window, drawing by F. Winton Newman, Architectural Association Sketchbook for 1904.

alternating shapes which these generate are reinforced by alternating patterns of cusping. Although the design as a whole is unique, its elements can all be paralleled at Christ Church and St Augustine's at Canterbury, in works attributed to Michael of Canterbury, the most important architect working in south-east England in the decades either side of 1300. The most striking single motif, used in an elementary form round some of the angels' busts inside the end wall of the north transept, is the spiky cusping known as Kentish or split cusping. Michael's masterpiece, St Stephen's Chapel in Westminster Palace, the English Sainte-Chapelle, was temporarily abandoned in 1297, around the same time as he must have been starting work on the magnificent tomb in the Abbey for Edmund, Earl of Lancaster. Beginning with Henry of Reyns, the Abbey's architect was usually also a leading royal architect of the day, a connection that continued, with intermissions, down to the Reformation. Inside the east walk, the most enterprising feature is the lierne vault over the chapter house entrance bay. Probably the only earlier lierne vault is that in the lower chapel of St Stephen's.

The Perpendicular Work

The south cloister walk and the outer parlour at its west end are all of a piece. In 1344 the foundations were being dug, in 1347 Abbot Byrcheston granted to the works of the cloister and parlour his revenues from St Edward's Fair, and by 1349 the vaulting was in hand. The south walk is much lower than the east walk, but like the south bays of the latter, this is extremely advanced work for its date. It is in

83

fact the oldest piece of Perpendicular architecture to have survived in the London area. The main lines of the window tracery, the diagnostic perpendiculars touching the framing arches, are authentic, though their cusping and fussy ironwork are by Scott. The cusping is probably a wrong guess for it is almost the only feature that is not a roughly one-and-a-half times enlargement of the cloister of Old St Paul's Cathedral, begun in 1332 to the designs of William Ramsey, chief royal architect from 1336 until his death in 1349 and originator of Perpendicular architecture in the south-east.

Unfortunately, the accounts relating to the south walk do not reveal the identity of the architect until 1352, by which time John Palterton was in charge. Since Palterton had worked under Ramsey on St Stephen's Chapel in 1344, and since the latter had supplied two tombs in the Abbey, including that of Abbot Henley (1344) it seems more than likely that Ramsey himself was responsible for this near-copy of his own masterwork at St Paul's. The simple tierceron vault is now very decayed, but bosses at each end once bore the initials of Nicholas Litlyngton, prior from 1349 and abbot from 1362. Probably it was these which led the fifteenth-century monk-historian, John Flete to atttribute the entire walk to Litlyngton.

Around 1970 parts of the vault shafts and window mullions were inaccurately renewed, and the Romanesque masonry of the back wall was cut out and replaced by machine-dressed ashlar. High up in the south wall of the eastern corner bay is a pair of openings which may possibly be connected with the refectory bell which hung somewhere nearby. A replica of c. 1970 of the towel cupboard is at the other end of the walk, its ogee reticulated tracery anomalous in an otherwise Perpendicular building. Next, in the western corner bay, is the door to the refectory, part of the remodelling carried out in 1305-6 by Robert the Mason. Its ogee label and cusping and the bossy foliage within the cusps recall work of about the same date at Norwich Cathedral. The only other part of the refectory seen by the public (most easily from the north cloister walk) is the north wall with Robert's simple two-light windows, now blocked. In line with the window wall of the south walk are wrought iron grilles echoing the fourteenth-century tracery. They were made in 1721-2 by Thomas Knight, no doubt to designs by William Dickinson.

The west walk, completed in 1365, is in the same style as the south walk, the main difference being that the windows have four lights and more tracery units. At the south end is the segmental arched lavatorium or washing place for the refectory, flanked by vault corbels vigorously carved as half figures of men in secular dress. Above the west processional door are blind tracery circles, some with the 'four-petal' design popularized by William Ramsey, others still with the pre-Perpendicular motif of interlocking mouchettes. The 'four-petal' motif recurs in the tympana over the lavatorium and between the vaults of the west and north walks.

THE CHAPTER HOUSE

The chapter house was begun at the same time as the church to which it is joined on its north-west side. In 1249 a lectern was ordered for it and in 1253 canvas was purchased as temporary filling for the windows. Almost as soon as it was finished, the king made it available as a meeting place for other bodies than the monks for whom it was primarily intended, and during the fourteenth century it became a frequent venue for the Commons. At the Dissolution the chapter house was retained by the Crown, and from the reign of Edward VI until 1866 it served as a repository for the records of the Exchequer and other Courts. The great windows were bricked up piecemeal from 1672-3, and the vault, long dangerous, was taken down in 1751-2. Since the completion of Scott's careful restoration of 1866-73, the chapter house has been an Ancient Monument in the care of the Office of Works and its successors.

The Vestibules

The entrance from the cloister consists of a low double doorway and a high sculptured tympanum, the whole enclosed in an arch of two orders filling one lunette of the cloister vault. For the sculpture see p. 95. The door arches themselves have a continuous hollow moulding decorated with widely spaced tufts of stiff leaf. The outer vestibule of the chapter house is very low so as to fit below the dormitory floor. This restriction in height and the need to keep the vault springings reasonably high account for the division into two aisles, for the shallow pitch of the vaults and for the use of strange near triangular arches like those on the outside of the gallery windows of the church. A staircase to the library filled the north aisle until 1866 and sheltered its vault bosses from weathering.

The inner vestibule houses the stairs leading up to the main room, which is raised above an undercroft. On the west wall is blind tracery almost identical to that in the north cloister walk. The north wall has two rather crudely detailed windows lending light to St Faith's chapel. In the south-east bay is a window of three cusped lancets with two pointed trefoils which Scott restored from fragments. If the reconstruction is correct, this is the earliest example of a design which became generally current only in the last decades of the thirteenth

The vault of the Chapter House.

century. The east wall is filled by the door to the chapter house proper. Its main arch is very like that from the cloister, but it encloses a double entrance treated like a two-light tracery window. Scott mistakenly filled the central quatrefoil with a relief sculpture that darkens the inner vestibule. The other face of the door is flanked by original sculptures of censing angels which turn away from the doors, as they would not have done had it contained an important image.

The Main Building

The main room of the chapter house is octagonal like that formerly at Beverley Minster, where there was also an undercroft. The grandest English Gothic chapter house earlier than Westminster is the ten-sided example at Lincoln, but whereas Lincoln is a wide room lit by relatively small lancets, Westminster is dominated by tall traceried windows which hoist the vault up to a new height and void the walls into huge glazed screens. Paradoxically, this distinctively English type of chapter house is Westminster's only wholehearted demonstration of the glass-cage aesthetic perfected in the clearstoreys of Amiens and St-Denis and at the Sainte-Chapelle. In one respect it goes further than any French building towards giving windows precedence over vaulting. The springings of the vault are exactly level with those of the window heads and so do not obstruct them when seen diagonally. This perfect visibility for the windows was most nearly matched at St-Denis, but there, as in all major churches, the wide span of the central vessel determines that the vaults spring well below the clearstorey window heads. At Westminster the distance from each angle to the central pier is not too much more than the width of each side, so the differently pitched arches and ribs spanning these distances can quite easily spring at the same level.

The tracery of the windows was accurately restored by Scott on the basis of the blind window against the south-east corner of the transept, which had survived the eighteenth-century alterations. The pattern is very like the side windows of the Sainte-Chapelle, but the whole design, including the unencircled quatrefoils, is an almost exact copy of windows in some of the chapels added to the nave of Notre-Dame in Paris around 1240. The heads of the windows are more richly moulded than they would have been in France and the jamb shafts are bulkier. This applies also to the Amiens- or St-Denis-inspired half-quatrefoil arcading above the wall benches. The diaper in the spandrels is exquisitely carved and very varied in design. On the east wall, where the abbot and other senior monks sat, the capitals are consistently stiff-leaf rather than moulded and the arcading has greater depth. The arches and spandrels here retain medieval polychromy, our best guide to the internal finish of the church.

The main entrance arch is flanked by two levels of blind arches, the upper pair housing an Annunciation group. The spandrels over the arch are occupied by irregular trefoils which require the angels within them to be of two sizes. Scott made the west window uniform with the rest, despite having found traces of a fourteenth-century replacement with five lights.

The vault is Scott's reconstruction, vouched for by the survival of original springers between the windows and on the central pier. Unlike the richly ribbed vault at Lincoln, Westminster lacks tiercerons and ridge ribs. The aim seems to have been to avoid competing with the windows. Similarly, the central pier obstructs the view of the windows as little as is compatible with its stability. An original feature which Scott, quite understandably, shrank from reinstating, was the series of iron tie bars radiating from the central pier to the peripheral vault springings. As Lethaby said, the effect must have been like the spokes of an umbrella. Scott was able to dispense with ties by suspending his vault from the iron structure of his high pitched outer roof.

The exterior is in its masonry entirely Scott's, though the design seems mostly authentic. The flying buttresses were added later, probably in 1377-8, to supplement original buttressing to the angles. The flyer nearest the church is Scott's, the original having been removed in 1707 to improve access to the south transept. The elaborately Decorated parapet and pinnacles are, needless to say, Scott's invention. All the pre-eighteenth-century views show a battlemented parapet without pinnacles and a low-pitched covering instead of Scott's Lincoln-inspired pyramid.

OTHER MONASTIC OFFICES

Buildings to the East of the Cloister

The Romanesque dormitory undercroft and the so-called Dark Cloister from which it is reached are discussed on p. 17. The northern third of the dormitory proper was converted into the library by Dean Williams in c. 1620 and can be seen by the public on Wednesdays.

A passage through the ground floor of the dormitory near its southern end leads to the infirmary cloister or Little Cloister, an attractive garden surrounded by segmental Portland stone arcades on rectangular piers. The arcades must date from c. 1681, the date on a ceiling in a house which stood over the south walk until the Second World War. The houses on both sides were built as prebendal residences. The westernmost houses on the north side are original, but the whole side was given a heavy cornice and pedimented dormers by Lord Mottestone in 1946-56. The more pretentious range beyond the east side of the cloister is also Mottestone's. The back walls of the cloister were built by John Palterton in 1364-7.

At the south-east corner is part of the eleventh-century reredorter, for which see p. 17. In the centre of the east side is the door to the infirmary chapel, built by Palterton in 1371-2. Its head and jambs are lined with quatrefoils, a pretty motif deriving ultimately from William Ramsey's presbytery of Lichfield Cathedral, begun in 1337. This door is opened on Thursdays to give a good view of the ruins of the mid-twelfth-century chapel (see p. 21). Before the 1298 fire, the chapel opened out of an infirmary hall in the conventional way.

Buildings to the West of the Cloister

In a line with the south walk of the cloister is the contemporary outer parlour. The residually Decorated windows here show Palterton's incomplete adherence to the Perpendicular of his erstwhile master, William Ramsey. The parlour is divided from the identically detailed entrance passage of the gatehouse by a relatively small door. Out of the north side of the west bay opens the entrance passage to the courtyard of the abbot's house. Except for occasional openings of the College Hall and Jerusalem Chamber, this is not shown to the public.

In the north-east corner of Dean's Yard is the front of the gatehouse, its details mostly modern invention. From here southwards runs the cellarer's building of *c.* 1388-91. In the mid-thirteenth-century its predecessor was against the west walk of the cloister; the relocation was presumably to allow more room for the abbot's house. The simple ground-floor windows are mostly restorations perpetuating what was there before. This is followed by the contemporary Blackstole Tower which now leads into a small Georgian courtyard but originally gave access to the monastic kitchen. The details of its tierceron vault are preserved only by the seventeenth- or eighteenth-century repairs in plaster. The heightened and Georgianized range which follows was taken over by the Abbey's Grammar School in 1461. Next, embedded in a fiercely Victorianized but structurally late fourteenth-century range, is the gateway to Little Dean's Yard, now occupied entirely by Westminster School. The entrance passage is again tierceron vaulted but in two bays and with slightly different details from those of the Blackstole Tower.

In Broad Sanctuary, overlapping the south tower of the west front, are the great chamber (Jerusalem Chamber) and great hall of the abbot's house completed by John Palterton in 1375. The north window of Jerusalem Chamber is early sixteenth-century, but the other windows are still of the original pattern: two lights under a hexagon enclosing four petal-like mouchettes. Against the west wall of the abbot's house is the abbey shop, built c.1880 as Chapter Offices and refenestrated in Georgian Gothic fashion in 1954-6 by S E Dykes Bower.

Chapter Five

THE EMBELLISHMENTS AND FURNISHING OF THE MEDIEVAL CHURCH

THE THIRTEENTH-CENTURY ARCHITECTURAL SCULPTURE

THE PROGRAMME of sculptural embellishment for the interior of Westminster Abbey was the richest ever undertaken in a medieval building of comparable dimensions, and every surviving fragment is worth seeking out. Both the wall arcading and the doorways of the transept ends are decorated with naturalistic leaves, which can also be seen in the earliest bosses. This motif originates from Reims and was first used in England in St Edward's Chapel in Windsor in 1243-4 under the direction of Henry of Reyns. The wall arcading along the south side of the eastern arm and transept is decorated with diapered spandrels. The north side is more ambitious in subject matter: spandrels in the northern chapels depict encounters between royal figures and angels; and in the north transept also show Samson and the lion, St Margaret and St Michael (opposite his chapel) and All Saints.

The higher sculpture of the internal elevations of the transept ends offers the observer rich rewards. At the third stage of the north transept the soffits of the six lancet windows carry roundels of musical angels. Some, more crisp than others, have been unjustly suspected of being nineteenth-century copies. The uneven condition of these figures was, however, noted in 1829, and is due to the varied resistance of the different stones to pollution and condensation. The frameworks of these relatively flat broad reliefs are stiff leaf, which indicates native workmanship. Against the return walls at either end

Western angel of a pair situated at high level on the south transept end wall.

are two standing kings, probably the Confessor and St Edmund.

Looking up to the fourth storey, the central spandrels are richly carved with stiff leaf, with blank strips for missing figures — their surviving companions are in the south transept. The corner half spandrels hold two great censing angels, only just less exciting than those opposite. No paint survives, though it does on the south side. Blandness here and in the angelic soffits may be due to Scott.

The thinner wall of the south transept means no soffit angels at the third register. Against a diapered ground in the fourth zone are two figures, one of them seated, his right hand eagerly outstretched. This must be Edward the Confessor at table, receiving back his ring, and with it news of his approaching death. The cloaked figure is therefore St John, so the northern pair were the Confessor giving his ring to the pilgrim. The two flanking angels are among the loveliest creations of medieval art: their lips are just parted in a smile, and their feet rest on a little lion or a stiff leaf, and they swing censors. The painted patterns on their draperies are in part original.

In the eastern nave the figure spandrels are replaced by a series of

LEFT: The hawk capital in a window splay of the muniment room. RIGHT AND OPPOSITE: The combat bosses of the south bay of the muniment room. RIGHT: Centaur and dragon.

shields of arms, each originally suspended by twin straps from head corbels. In 1254 Henry III was entertained in the Palace of the Old Temple in Paris, where, 'according to continental custom were hung up as many bucklers as the walls would hold'. The first English Rolls of Arms *c.*1255 begin with sovereigns and continue with English earls, lords and knights — just what we have here. The 'General Roll' of the nave spandrels starts at the east end of both aisles, with Edward the Confessor and the Holy Roman Emperor, followed by the Kings of England and France, and behind them a company, processing in pairs towards the altar.

When the nave was completed in the later fourteenth century, the original series of shields was continued, this time only in paint. The designers must have had access to the thirteenth-century Roll which continued to be the blueprint. Perhaps this commemorated those who contributed to the building of the Abbey, in response to a Papal Indulgence of 1249/50. As well as the Roll of Arms, other earlier material was used when works were resumed after a century: at least two, and probably more thirteenth-century head stops, as well as several pendant beasts which were probably meant for external pinnacles, can be recognized in the later fourteenth-century arcading. Clearly the work had closed down abruptly in 1272, with sculpture already prepared for the following season.

Some of the finest sculptural decoration has been lavished in the small space known as the muniment room in the south west angle of the south transept over the cloister. Here are three of the best

LEFT: Man and dragon. RIGHT: Man and half-man-half-beast.

preserved and most exciting bosses of the Abbey, the splendid 'Mythical Combats', describing men, centaurs and dragons locked in mortal strife. Their head types include the furrowed brow found in the nave spandrels and stops and in Henry III's own effigy. The 1253 account included 32 shillings for four bosses to Robert of Beverley who was to succeed as master mason in 1260 and was to be paid for the wax effigy of Henry III in 1272.

In the thirteenth century this space may have been used either as a royal pew, or as a partially hidden gallery for singing boys, a custom from the tenth century documented elsewhere. The transept ends are alive with sculpted angels, censing or making music. Their visual Epiphany was surely complemented by the 'Vox Angeli'. Probably at the behest of the efficient Abbot Nicholas de Litlyngton, the space was converted in the late fourteenth century to its present purpose of a muniment room. The floor was tiled, and a tall record cupboard installed against an inserted wooden partition. This was decorated on its north side with a large painting of the White Hart, lying in a bed of Rosemary for Remembrance, the badge of Richard II. The painting, of heraldic simplicity, is just visible from below.

The English carvers' special skills in this kind of figurative work would have been wasted on the main vault bosses, which are too high to be appreciated, so in the Abbey these are exclusively foliate. As well as natural and standard stiff leaves, a larger, undulated stiff leaf was evolved here in response to the challenge of legibility. The biggest and waviest example of this appears on the tympanum of

93

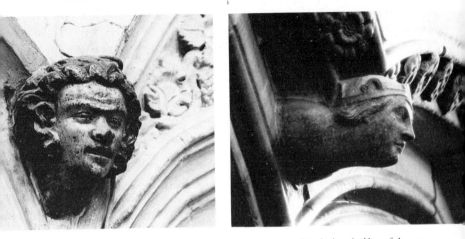

LEFT: Negro head-stop of the thirteenth century incorporated in the later building of the nave. RIGHT: The 'Prince Edward' head-stop inside the north transept entrance.

the door from the cloister to the monks' dormitory (now the library), part of Henry III's campaign.

Nearer the eye, in the west aisle of the transepts, there was a fine series of bosses of religious subjects, including David harping, Aaron and Moses, the Virgin and Child, the Annunciation, the Assumption, and souls in Abraham's bosom. Unfortunately these bosses are of the more perishable stone, and only traces of their original beauty remain. The wide array of Tudor emblems on the bosses of the western nave declare how long it took to complete the building.

The vigour and variety of thirteenth-century sculpture is particularly evident in the head corbels, of which the most important collections are within the gallery of the eastern arm (not open to the public) and in the Chapel of St Faith. Here Westminster sculpture is at its closest to that of Reims. In the chancel of St Faith's Chapel notice the 'dreaming youth' to the north, and the smiling lady opposite him. Others include a monk, heads in distress, and a very striking negro head — there are others in St Benedict's Chapel and in the nave. This motif occurred at Reims, and once established at Westminster spread to Lincoln, Wells, Salisbury, York and Gloucester.

Do not miss the spurs at the bases of the crossing piers. These are decorated with leaves, a fashion long established in England. The north-west pier has monkeys' or dragons' heads, and the north-east a lion attacking a horse.

The inner entrance to the chapter house, with Scott's interpolated Christ blacked out to show how the original disposition may have been. The circle would have been cusped.

The Chapter House

The entrance to the chapter house from the east walk of the cloister is surmounted by the largest surviving thirteenth-century tympanum in England. From Burges' watercolour in the Victoria and Albert Museum, and from Lethaby's loving study a glimpse of the full effect can be appreciated — in good light something can still be made out. There were three tall figures against a background of trails of gilt foliage on a blue ground. The presiding figure was the Virgin carrying her Child, framed by a canopy almost as slender as that painted round St Faith in her chapel. The fragments now on her pedestal were not there in 1820. She was supported by two angels, of which the southern one still speaks. There are three series of 'ancestors' in the voussoirs of this and the inner doorway — at Amiens also they were repeated. On the inner doorway, the side towards the vestibule had a rose with the Virgin at the apex, the one within included Moses, with Christ as the keystone.

Two stiff-leaf bosses in the vestibule of the chapter house.

The iconography of the inner doorway is gravely distorted by Scott's interpolated Christ. The doorway stands for Mary's acceptance of the Incarnation. The angels in the trefoils around the door are extra attendants upon that event: Gabriel and Mary of the Annunciation, either side of the entrance on the inside, are among the most beautiful survivors of Henry III's Abbey. They are associated with a payment of 53/4 to William Ixeworth in 1253, but might be by different carvers. The Mary has the weakly curling fingers of the David harping boss in the north transept aisle. All the innovations of style are in the Gabriel, whose expressive but eccentric anatomy recalls the wall arcading fragments in the museum. A single slot behind his right shoulder took a wing, no doubt of metal, and large enough to cover the lack of a second. Both figures have a dark coating, possible of shellac; the angel is chalk, probably from Tottenhoe, and she is of Reigate stone. Mary was found by Scott in 1842 behind the panelling; the angel was already standing in the vestibule. The rest of the doorway carving is largely original, or very carefully pieced in — look out for lions. The wall arcading has been largely renewed, except for the dragon rebate in the recess in the east wall. Scott's vault may incorporate some original bosses.

THE LITURGICAL FURNISHINGS

The greater medieval churches had a double focus: an enclosed choir for the maintainance of the daily services; and a Shrine beyond it, to which pilgrims flocked to pay homage. At Westminster there is a third focus, the Coronation. The choir and sanctuary at Westminster were originally closed off from the public, who went round them to reach the Shrine. The veneration of the remains of St Edward the Confessor is perpetually witnessed by the company of Kings and Queens buried around him. They occupy every reasonable — and unreasonable — space. There has been jostling for position, and lesser men, such as Eltham and de Valence have been pushed aside. The links are now closed in a tight golden chain of history around the Shrine itself and the Coronation Chair.

On the historical occasions of Coronations, massive scaffolding is erected across the exceptionally wide transepts, giving the laity tolerable visibility of those parts of the proceedings which take place under the crossing. The special duty of the sanctuary at Westminster is to witness the Sacramental aspect of the consecration of kings on earth, as the special duty of the Confessor's Chapel is to be their threshold to a heavenly kingdom; and of the choir to maintain an unbroken cycle of prayer for the good of the kingdom.

It is only through a recognition of these three strands — the monastic core, the Confessor's Shrine and the setting for coronations — that we can understand the furnishings and works of art. All three of these religious purposes were served by the furnishings, especially by those unique to the Abbey; for example those executed by the Italian School of the Cosmati who relaid classical Roman columns and marbles in combination with mosaic fragments (which may have also been recycled) for floors and liturgical furnishings with symbolic geometric repeat designs. The Sanctuary floor, the floor of the Confessor's Chapel, the Shrine base, the base of the tomb altar in the south aisle at the east end, the tomb of Henry III himself and the de Valence tomb slabs were carried out by the Cosmati during the later part of the reign of Henry III and that of his successor Edward I, and were completed by 1291 at the latest.

Edward I was in Sicily in 1271-2, and his exposure to Monreale and Apulia may have influencd the design of the last of these, Henry III's tomb base. He is known to have brought back further materials from Jerusalem. The Sanctuary floor (1268) and the Shrine base (1269 or 1279) are signed by Italian craftsmen. Westminster Cosmati work differs from Italian in that the matrix is dark Purbeck instead of Carrara marble, giving the effect of a negative.

The Cosmati Floors

The Sanctuary floor, like the one in the crypt of Anagni cathedral which was consecrated in 1255, could be used as a liturgical map for processions. The significance of the pattern takes on a further dimension when the particular rite to be performed in this place was the anointing, consecration and crowning of kings, with a throne in the centre.

Working from the outside towards the centre, the triple design of the floor consists of a square with a wide border enclosing a second square set diamond-wise, with four circles in the four angles between the squares. Within the second square is a circle of no greater diameter than the outer four, with four smaller circles on the four compass points. Thanks to the fifteenth-century Westminster historian, Richard Sporley, we have a record of the triple inscription that encircled the design.

Around the inner border of the large square a few letters of the inscription, laid in brass letters of Lombardic script, survive. Starting along the eastern edge from the left hand side, it may be roughly translated: 'In the year of Christ one thousand, two hundred and seventy two less four King Henry the third, Odericus of the City and the Abbot of this place assembled here these porphry stones'. Although this inscription was probably not cut into the pavement until Henry III's death in 1272, it confirms that the pavement was laid in 1268. Richard Ware, who became Abbot in 1258, became papal chaplain the following year. He visited Anagni several times, once in 1267. The papal curia was in residence there. In 1269 Ware received £50 from the king for 'the pavement which be brought with him from the Court of Rome to the King's use to be put in the Church at Westminster before the King's great altar there . . .'

The second inscription was carried round the quatrefoil formed by the four circles round the inner square. It was made in a continuous band of brass, and has entirely gone. It described a method of calculating the end of the world. Some parts survive of the innermost inscription running round the central circle. It may be translated: 'Here the sphere points to the microcosm, the globe to the archetype', and alludes to the cosmic significance of the pavement and the coronation ritual performed upon it.

Most of the patterns, carried out in the widest range of coloured marbles, with inlays that included glass, can be made out with the help of old records, of which Ackerman's watercolour is the most informative. The liturgical significance, however, was soon lost, as it was covered with a cloth of gold as early as Edward I's Coronation.

The Cosmati pavement of the Confessor's Chapel was laid in 1267. It is composed of over two hundred intertwined circles, designed to reach the first of the four steps to the Shrine as originally laid, and co-

Henry III's tomb from the aisle showing the Cosmati work on the base.

ordinated with the base of Henry III's tomb. The circles are differentiated with a variety of interlocked patterns, some of them based on triangles. The best idea of what this pavement — inevitably concealed — looks like can be gained by an examination of the altar tomb in the south ambulatory.

The High Altar Screen

The present altar screen, the second in this position, was completed in 1440-1 to the design of John Thirsk, warden of the masons at Westminster Abbey from 1420, and also responsible for the Chantry of Henry V. The Islip Roll portrays the high altar, the western side. The main register was punctuated around the doors by canopied niches containing figures. The centre pair was a bishop and a king.

A scene from the life of the Confessor from the frieze on the east side or back of the High Altar Screen.

Above them there was a rood loft, itself in two tiers: the lower part housed the hanging pyx, flanked by figures of St Peter with tiara and St Paul with his sword; and above these was the Rood itself with Mary and John flanked by Cherubim on wheels.

The disposition of the centre part of the reredos is alas concealed in the Islip Roll by the superimposition of funereal hangings —bearing, no doubt, the arms of Abbot Islip. The altar piece itself was also covered with a cloth bearing a representation of the Crucifixion in the centre, thus depriving us of our only chance of seeing the medieval altar piece through early sixteenth-century eyes. However, since the centre area of the reredos is today of the same proportions as the retable itself, we must assume that Gilbert Scott retained these proportions in filling this space with J R Clayton's mosaic of the Last Supper.

The side of the reredos facing the Confessor's Chapel is relatively complete except for the standing figures. The arrangement of the centre echoed that on the other side, with two groups of figures flanking the doors. The canopy work, where it survives, has sophisticated miniature fan vaulting with pendants, tilted to reveal the patterning. A complete frieze of small scenes from the life of the Confessor survives here; the sculpture is weathered, and the detail largely blunted but the poses and draperies are carefully worked and dramatic. The scenes are punctuated by trefoils which are also used in the frieze in the Chapel of Henry V, for which Thirsk was responsible.

The Retable

Although its importance had been recognized by George Vertue in 1736 and later by Horace Walpole and the antiquarian artists Jacob Schnebbelie and John Carter, in 1827 Edward Blore found the retable, the greatest single survival of the Abbey's medieval furnishings, lying on top of a pile of cases together with the equally neglected royal funerary effigies in the upper Islip Chapel. The right hand end of it had been painted white, to harmonize with one of the eighteenth-century marble tombs.

The exact date of the Westminster Retable is fiercely contested, but it is generally agreed that it was the altarpiece over the High Altar of Henry III's newly rebuilt Sanctuary. The reasons for this identification are threefold: its dimensions tally with those now occupied by Gilbert Scott's altarpiece, set into the framework of the 1440 screen (it is argued that the Retable was transferred to a new setting in 1440); its iconographic scheme is totally appropriate to the high altar — it celebrates the Titular Saint, paired with St Paul, accompanying Christ as Creator carrying the world, with Eucharistic reference in the narrative scenes; and its quality is superb. Against this evidence some have argued that the High Altar itself, one of the two most precious focuses of all of Henry III's glittering assembly, could not have included simulation jewels. This is to forget the last stage of Henry III's patronage of the Abbey, when the king pressed on despite grave financial difficulties that had led him, as near the consecration date as 1267, to pawn the chief jewels from the shrine itself. Henry's financial difficulties were increased by disloyalty, perhaps also by embezzlement, and eventually by the untimely death of his chief goldsmith, William of Gloucester, in 1269.

The Retable was complemented by a magnificent altar frontal which took three women nearly four years to make. Upon a foundation of waxed canvas was applied a 'design in gold thread using white pearls to the tune of £71 and great pearls £12.13s.4d; seven hundred and eighty six enamels in the borders, and seventy six large enamels, five hundred and fifty garnets in the borders in gold settings . . . '.

The borders of the Retable itself are made up in constantly repeated panels including the motif of the castle of Castile against a green ground, referring to the marriage between Henry's son, the future Edward I and Eleanor of Castile in 1254. They were painted and then covered with glass, giving the effect of enamelling. There is provison within the borders for twenty-four cameos of heads, of which only one, thirteenth-century imitation cameo survives, plus one oval filled with red glass, perhaps once a base for gesso. Above and below the central part of the Retable are six larger recesses, long ovoid rectangles, designed for outsize cameos, intaglios or precious stones. We can appreciate something of the effect intended by visiting the encrusted Pala d'Oro at St Mark's in Venice, which was refurbished in the early thirteenth and early fourteenth centuries.

The record of Edward of Westminster in search of a single cameo for the shrine in 1251 gives us a glimpse of the way Henry set about such a task. The basic framework of the shrine was organized in 1241, and presumably contained many blanks with dummy embellishments, which Henry hoped to replaced with real gems. It would seem that the Retable was built in the same way and was put in place without a full collection of antique gems. At the Reformation, of course, it would have been systematically despoiled of genuine stones, and only the dummies remained.

The patterned background behind the gable on the left once more connects with the early thirteenth-century parts of the Pala d'Oro, while that behind the right hand gable is more Islamic. The borders of the garments of St Peter and St John and smaller figures in the paintings are ornamented with Cufic motifs. Traffic in exotic materials and influences is well recorded at Westminster: in 1241 a tunical and dalmatic were made for Henry III from 'cloth of Musc' given to him by his uncle, Peter of Savoy, whilst in 1252 William of Gloucester, the king's goldsmith, furnished more than one hundred 'oboli de Musc' for the shrine.

The central figures in the Retable painting represent Christ flanked by the Virgin and St John. Where an earthly king would be carrying an orb, the standing Christ holds the globe of the world, on which can be made out the earth, with trees and plants growing upon it, birds and grazing amimals and a boatman rowing on the water below. According to thirteenth-century cosmology, there was only solid ground on the 'upper' surface of the globe: the 'underside' was occupied by the waters 'that are beneath the earth' and the sky was circumscribed by the arc of the 'firmament of heaven'. The orb in Christ's hand therefore represents the universe in elevation and cross section. The significance of the orb is linked to the innermost circle of the sanctuary Cosmati floor.

Mary and John carry palms of martyrdom: according to the Golden Legend Mary received, as token of her impending death, a palm which she passed miraculously to John. There is a deliberate parallel with the

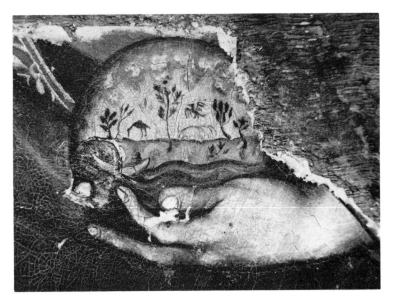

*The globe in the hand of Christ in the centre of the Retable. Observe the waters
above the firmament and fish in the waters beneath the earth. See the beasts grazing, the birds
and the little man in his boat under the light of the moon — all within the space of
a small coin.*

returning of the ring to Edward the Confessor here, since the pilgrim
to whom Edward had given the ring was St John in disguise. As early
as 1243 Henry III had ordered an embroidered banner, of red samite
embroidered with gold with the images of Mary and John, to be
placed near the altar, which was made by the famous needlewoman,
Mabel of Bury St Edmunds.

The single figure at the left hand end of the reredos represents St
Peter carrying the keys of Heaven and Hell. The lost corresponding
figure from the other end was described by Vertue as St Paul with his
sword upright. Ultra-violet light and infra-red photography confirm
that there is the outline of a figure bearing either a sceptre or a sword
here, and both Peter and Paul are enthroned on the Abbey Ad
Causum Seal of *c.* 1400. The Abbey Church was dedicated to St Peter
— Paul was the dedication of the East Minster, St Paul's. His prominence in the iconography of the Abbey can be easily explained by the
relics. Edward the Confessor had given the Abbey a whisker from St
Peter's beard, but a much more important relic of St Paul: the maniple
in which it was claimed his decapitated head had been wrapped. This
will have been the focal point of the Chapel of St Paul to the north of
the shrine.

LEFT: Second Seal of Henry III c. 1259, designed by William of Gloucester. RIGHT: Seal ad causam of Abbot Ware dated 1268.

The long, sinuous figures of the Westminster Retable, with their tight curls and concave poses, their silky draperies in muted tones and their refined gestures, appear in several other works: the lost painting of the Coronation of the Confessor in the Painted Chamber, virtually documented to 1267; the Douce Apocalypse, of before 1272; and the little Ad Causam seal of Abbot Richard Ware, dated 1268. The Confessor, though only two centimetres high, has here all the curvaceous grace of the Retable. This seal was probably produced at the Westminster workshops by the king's goldsmith, William of Gloucester.

Between the elegant figure of St Peter and the central group there are four painted scenes, described by Vertue as Miracles of the New Testament. On the upper left is the raising of Jairus' daughter, with the hand of Christ taking the little hand of the child, her splendid pillow, the fur lining of her bedclothes, and anxious parents and attendant disciples. In the next scene the figure of the stooping Christ drawing in a square of dust, and the long golden hair of the woman taken in adultery are clear. The edge of a hilly landscape is all that remains of the lower left hand subject — we may guess the Transfiguration or the Raising of Lazarus. The scene on the bottom right is the Feeding of the Five Thousand, with its Eucharistic reverberances. The astonished disciples are on the left, the eager crowd on the right, even the boy handing up his loaves and fishes is there — only the central figure of Christ blessing the loaves is missing.

Of the pendant series of subjects on the other side of the Retable we know nothing more, though we may expect them to have included the Turning of Water into Wine at Cana (to pair with the Feeding of the Five Thousand). The borders of St Peter's and St John's cloaks and

LEFT: *Later thirteenth-century painting of St Faith in her Chapel.* RIGHT: *The sedilia on the south side of the sanctuary, 1308.*

of the figures in the miracle scenes are ornamented with floriated Cufic motifs.

In addition to Master William, the Westminster monk 'his beloved painter', Henry III attracted artists in all media and of all nationalities to his works at Westminster — William of Florence, John of St Omer, and Peter de Hispania. The last of these was already working in 1253, and in 1272 was paid for two 'well painted tables' for the Altar of St Mary, valued at the large sum of £80. The Islamic features in the Retable suggest this artist, but nationality was of small importance: all Henry's chief artists had been working at Westminster for at least fifteen years by 1268 and were citizens of the specific artistic environment of Westminster rather than of any particular country. Neither Spain nor Florence could have taught the Westminster Retable Master much — by 1268 he would have been a leader in the skills of courtly refinement in any court. The Westminster Retable, for all its wounded condition, is the finest panel painting of its time in Western Europe. Henry III's enterprise might have run out of funds to complement the painting with antique gems, but there was no exhaustion in the hand of his painter.

The Sedilia

In the mid-thirteenth century, the monks 'discovered' the remains of their legendary founder, King Sebert, and in 1308 his tomb was brought from the cloister to a new position on the south side of the High Altar. Over it were constructed the sedilia, a row of seats for the celebrant and his assistants at High Mass, which were the contribution of Abbot Walter Wenlock, probably buried just below them.

The sedilia are an elegant example of the 'ciborium' architecture of the tombs opposite it, but carried out this time in wood. The head stops of two young kings and a bishop or mitred abbot retain their full colour. The paintings surviving behind the seats are of two kings flanking an ecclesiastic, of whom only the lower part remains, perhaps St Peter. The background of the painting of the younger king is powdered with leopards, indicating that he was an Englishman, possibly Seabert.

The subjects of the four panels of the back and that over the low arch sheltering the tomb of Seabert are known, though the damage is no less extensive than at the front of the sedilia. To the east there was an Annunciation, and beside it Edward the Confessor holding out his ring to an (effaced) pilgrim. The painting of these panels is in the large, bold style of the Saints Christopher and Thomas wall paintings. The canopy is embellished with sprays of flowers like those on the Crouchback and Aveline tombs. The gables were originally set with red and blue glass, and even the slightest and leanest space is articulated with painted tracery or simulated ashlar.

The Coronation Chair

There are two essential parts of the English Coronation Service as it has been carried out for time immemorial, and in the Abbey since 1066: the Anointing, Investiture and Crowning of the Sovereign — the Sacramental Coronation, carried out by the Lords Spiritual; and the Enthronement and Homage, where the Lords Temporal and the Third Estate play their part. The first part was an almost private occasion, especially during the Middle Ages, when sovereigns of both sexes were stripped to the waist for the Anointing, as well as 'grovelling' before the High Altar on specially arranged cushions. For the second part a stage was erected in the Middle Ages beneath the crossing, which not only gave the best possible view of their enthroned monarch to the largest possible number of people, but simultaneously made an effective barrier for the first, private, part by shutting off the sanctuary from the vulgar gaze. The royal seat upon this stage from

Detail of the scene of the raising of Jairus' daughter: Christ taking the hand of the little girl from the Retable.

which the sovereign received homage was properly called the Throne.

The Coronation Chair on the other hand, was set up in the centre of the sanctuary for the secret, sacramental, aspect of the coronation. When not in use it has resided between the High Altar and the Shrine ever since it was made in 1300-1.

In 1296 Edward I captured from the Scots, the Stone of Scone, which claimed many derivations, one from Egypt, with Moses foretelling that victory would follow it. It is of Old Red Sandstone, of a type found in the neighbourhood of Scone. It weighs about four hundredweight (990 kilos) and measure 26½in by 16½in by 11in (67cm by 42cm by 28cm). Iron rings were fixed into it, perhaps by Edward I, for ease of transport. At Scone in 1249 Alexander III was enthroned upon the stone itself 'according to ancient custom', but Edward I planned from the first to incorporate it into a chair, which he originally meant to have made of metal. This wooden chair was made under the direction of the King's Painter, Master Walter of Durham, and cost one hundred shillings. It was first used for the coronation of Edward II in 1308 and has been used by every crowned monarch since, though in the case of William and Mary, equally crowned, a replica was made which is now in the Abbey Museum. The earlier Mary I was so worried that the crowning of her Protestant half-brother, Edward VI, had cancelled the sanctity of the chair that she had a new one blessed for her by Pope Julius III, which she used for her anointing. This is now at Winchester, where it was used again for her wedding. The Coronation Chair was taken as far as Westminster Hall in 1657 for the installation as Lord Protector of Oliver Cromwell, who chose to use this rather than the King's Bench, the proper and ancient seat for the election by the Lords Temporal. During the Second World War the Chair was stored for safety in the crypt of Gloucester Cathedral, although the Stone was secreted in the Abbey.

Henry III was fully alert to the symbolic importance of thrones. 'Because we recall to memory that you told us' he wrote to Edward of Westminster in 1245, the year of the beginning of the great church, 'it would be more magnificent to make two bronze leopards (the heraldic term for lions) to be placed on either side of our throne at Westminster, than to make them out of chiselled or sculpted marble, we command you to get them made in metal as you told us . . .'. As Francis Wormald demonstrated, lions are the proper accompaniment to the throne of Solomon, and hence to all seats of wisdom. From the tenth century the antiphon of Zadok the Priest and Nathan the Prophet anointing Solomon King has been part of the English Coronation Ritual. There were probably lions (now sawn off) on the ends of the Coronation Chair, since Master Walter was paid 13s. 4d. for making and painting them. An enthroned king was represented on the inside of the back, with his foot upon a lion, as drawn by John Carter and William Burges. It was the main feature of the embellishments in gilded and pounced gesso, of which a reticulated pattern inside each arm, enclosing animals or birds among oak foliage survive. The external sides of the arms are panelled, and so is the back. Each panel contains a design of naturalistic leaves: thorn, ivy, vine and maple have been identified. The spandrels at the heads of these panels contained glass inlays over sprays painted on a metal ground. Traces of inscriptions were found when the Chair was examined in 1953.

The wonder is not that this delicate ornamentation is so damaged, but that any part of it remains. The first evidence of mutilation comes from the Coronation of Mary I, that uneasy occasion. Because she used her new chair for the Anointing and Crowning, she used this one for the Enthroning and Homage. Two lions of gold were attached to the back by way of additional emphasis — the clumsy peg holes remain. Cloth of gold coverings were nailed on to the chair for several coronations, and scars remain. In 1821 the pinnacles were sawn off, and the last remaining shield stolen from the grille enclosing the stone. For Queen Victoria's Jubilee Service in 1887 the Chair was painted dark brown, and subsequently scraped down again.

The lions on which the Chair so appropriately rests have had a poor press. As part of the preparation for the coronation of George II, Richard Roberts sent in a bill in 1717 for four new carved lions and an oak frame. From his account it would seem we owe the stretcher to Richard Roberts as well. It is likely that he copied lions already there — perhaps Tudor ones.

Since the back of the Chair represented the king enthroned, it was a symbol of his continuing presence. This idea also goes back to Henry III, who in 1250 commissioned a royal seat in the middle of the high table in the hall of Windsor — painted with 'an image of the king holding a sceptre in his hand . . . suitably adorned with painting in gold . . .'.

Edward III's sword and shield are kept by the Coronation Chair. It is thought that the sword is of German make, and was carried processionally before the King.

The Portrait of Richard II

The life-size panel of Richard II is the first such image which not only represented the monarch, but also looked like him. It follows the

LEFT: *A portrait of Richard II in full regalia, probably painted in 1396. RIGHT: The Coronation chair in the Confessor's Chapel, made to incorporate the Stone of Scone in 1308.*

mid-fourteenth-century cycle of life-like royal images in the Great Hall of the Castle of Karlsteyn made for the Emperor Charles VI, with whom Richard II was linked by his marriage to Anne of Bohemia. This portrait is not so much a record of his temporal appearance as an image of the presence of his Majesty. Its purpose was to represent the person of the King in his absence from the choir. Richard and his Queen did sit in the choir with the monks, and his visits to the Abbey were met by spectacular liturgy. He impaled his arms with those of the Confessor.

The shape of Richard's face, with prominent heavy-lidded eyes and double goatee beard, should be compared with his effigy. There is no more convincing portrait of a monarch of this date. It was undoubtedly taken from the appearance of Richard II as he was in 1396, aged 29, rather than at his coronation, when he was aged 11. Compare the fashion for claw-like hands with the illumination of him in the *Liber Regalis*. Richard's robes are scattered with the crowned 'R' that survives on so many rings. The gold background was treated in high relief gesso patterning until nineteenth-century 'restoration' scraped off all but one patch. Apparently it had gone before George Richmond restored the painting in 1866, but there is an old photograph in which it appears.

The panel can be dated to 1396, when there is a payment to Master Peter, Sacrist, for items to do with the monument to Queen Anne, 'and for the picture of a certain image portrayed in the similitude of a king in the choir of the church'.

OTHER WORKS OF ART

The Medieval Glass

Although the tally of medieval glass in the Abbey is tragically short, it is well worth hunting out. That in the three east windows of the main apse of the clearstorey was assembled by Sir Christopher Wren after 1700; some additional pieces are dated 1702 and 1706. The central figures represent, appropriately, St Edward the Confessor and the Pilgrim (the king's head is renewed), and come from the south west window of the nave near the west door to the cloister. Among glass which has been moved again are the shields of arms of England, Edward the Confessor, Richard Earl of Cornwall, and Provence (for Henry III's wife Eleanor): this is all now in St Edmund's Chapel. These pieces all date from Henry III's building period, and the arms recur in the nave arcade spandrels. Sandford recorded the arms of Henry III and Eleanor of Castile in the north transept glazing. Lethaby found some grisaille glass, and quoted the 1253 records for white and coloured glass, purchased from Laurence, glazier, and Richard Boser, white at 4d a foot, coloured 8d. He concluded that some of the glazing was grisaille, with shields of arms.

In 1708 Hatton recorded a series of single figures, including a Richard II in the nave south clearstorey. The figures now under the north and south towers at the west end are partial reminders of this scheme — the southern one is called the Black Prince.

There is a series of small scenes set in various oval and foiled shapes against blue backgrounds in the Jerusalem Chamber. These show the Massacre of the Innocents and a saint — possibly St Nicholas — and the false pilgrim in pointed ovals; the martyrdoms of St John the Baptist or St Alban, and that of St Stephen, both in pointed ovals with foiled sides; and the Descent of the Holy Ghost and Ascension, in mirror-image assymmetrical shapes. The narratives concerning John the Baptist and St Nicholas probably originally came from their ambulatory chapels; the Massacre of the Innocents may have come from the Chapel of St Nicholas (the patron saint of children) — the Abbey had relics 'of the small bones of the Innocents'. Part of a Resurrection in a roundel is in the muniment room. Small scale scenes like these are unlikely to have been intended for the clearstorey, where they would have been almost indecipherable.

The Wall Paintings

In her Chapel is the wall painting of St Faith, whose major shrine was at Conques and who was also the patronness of the crypt chapel of St Paul's Cathedral. Tall and remote, she bears the gridiron of her martyrdom. Her feet stand upon a painted corbel which supports the impossibly slender shafts of her painted canopy. Beneath her runs a reredos also painted upon the wall. In the centre of it is a Crucifixion, and on either side a pair of eight pointed star patterns, such as we see on the Retable. Their subjects are indecipherable. The soffit of the arch around the whole is decorated with chevrons, interrupted on the north side by an elongated barbed quatrefoil, in which kneels a Benedictine monk, praying to St Faith. His prayer translates: 'From the burden of my sore transgressions, sweet Virgin, deliver me; Make my peace with Christ and blot out my iniquity' . . .

This painting is likely to have been by Master William 'the King's beloved painter', a Westminster monk who was working in the Palace in 1256 and on a cross belonging to the Infirmary in 1259 and who appears in the accounts from c.1240 to 1280. Several features of this, the first painting on this wall, echo the Retable: the little windows on the pinnacles of St Faith's canopy, the 'comma' crockets, the exaggeration and elongation of the figure of St Faith. The painting has the faint glimmer of an oil-based technique, and accounts for Master William's work include materials which could have been used for this — eggs, wine, oil and varnish. The painting should be contemporary with the Retable, c.1270.

The wall paintings in the blind arcading of the south transept were only discovered in 1936 when the monuments to John Gay (d. 1732) and Nicholas Rowe (d.1718) were moved from Poet's Corner. Painted direct onto an inside wall, they have not yet come to harm from Professor Tristram's wax treatment. A striking aspect of these two paintings is their concentration on the exchange between the two figures: the fixed gaze of St Christopher dwelling on the Christ Child; the almost fierce regard of the Christ as he forces the arm of the reluctant and nervous Thomas into his wounded side. These are inter-relationships we would expect in work from Giovanni Pisano or Giotto, but nowhere north of the Alps, and such drama is not repeated in the vacant images of most English early fourteenth-century art.

The relatively delicate colours for the figures, set against the foil of a darker ground recalls Queen Mary's Psalter. The same preference is shown in the weepers of the Tomb of John of Eltham and is associated with the Pucelle Manuscripts or with Giotto.

In the late Middle Ages, St Christopher, the patron saint of travellers, was to become one of the most popular of all saints. No country church was complete without his gigantic outline, so placed on a north wall that he could be immediately seen from the door. This painting in the south transept may be the first wall painting of him in England. The lettering in the background is in Lombardic script, and its presence shows that c. 1300 Christopher was not generally familiar. By 1450 the mermaid at his feet in the water, or one of his giant toes, would have been enough for recognition. Christopher appears in an earlier drawing among the three added to the Westminster Psalter in the middle years of the thirteenth century, which is possibly his first isolated appearance in English art. Henry III gave the Abbey a relic of part of his head, and the saint's popularity spread steadily, perhaps from here.

Another relic is connected with the painting of St Thomas: the arm of the saint, given to the Abbey by the Confessor himself. No representation of Doubting Thomas more vividly demonstrates where his arm had been — right into the wounded side of Christ. Perhaps this painting suggests that the arm of St Thomas deserved exceptional veneration.

The green and red alternation for the backgrounds of these two wall paintings indicates the turn of the thirteenth century. Blue and red were predominant in the taste of Henry III's time. The greens and golds came in as techniques for stained glass developed, which by 1300 also favoured pale figures against rich backgrounds.

The wall arcading of the chapter house was treated with a cycle of paintings in the later fourteenth and early fifteenth centuries, partly at the expense of one of the monks, John of Northampton. They may have been painted in celebration of the eviction of the Commons. The central bays, where the Abbot and his senior officials presided, carry a Last Judgement, with Christ himself immediately behind the Abbot. Although they are now much damaged, we can see that these figures were probably impressive — they should be compared with those in the Byward Tower, and those originally in St Stephen's Chapel. The painting of the Apocalypse, which is busily laid out in registers round the rest of the walls, is disappointing. The dado, with an array of beasts including differentiated camel and dromedary, is a remarkable survival — the monks can't have leant back in their seats!

The Tiled Pavements

Both the chancel of the Chapel of St Faith and the muniment room were tiled in the fourteenth century, but the most ambitious tiled floor in England is the thirteenth-century floor still in place in the chapter house. This was completed in 1259 — when the remainder of the tiles were handed over to the Chapel of St Dunstan under the Dormitory (now the Pyx Chapel) — and was discovered and relaid, with a few replacements, by Scott when he lifted the wooden floor that had protected it for four centuries.

The bulk of the floor is laid out in strips, like the more modest pavement from the Queen's Chamber at Clarendon Palace which is now in the British Museum. Repeat patterns, usually made up of four tiles, are divided by borders of magnificent stiff leaf or St Peter's fish. The rose window pattern probably reflects the north transept rose window in its original glory. The Royal Arms are supported by centaurs. The only comparable tiles, the Tristram series now in the British Museum, were also made under Henry III's patronage.

Nothing is made of the central pillar in the floor as arranged, but we do not know how much adjustment Scott may have made. Portions of a sixteen-tile centralized pattern which could have surrounded the pillar have been found among the miscellaneous tiles on the south side. The placing of the tomb of Edward the Confessor's Abbot, Edwin, near the south wall accounts for the confusion there — perhaps some of the single tiles in that area were originally in the vestibule which Scott retiled. Among these is the inscribed strip which Lethaby deciphered: 'As the rose is among flowers, so is this house among houses. King Henry, friend of the Holy Trinity, dedicated it to Christ who loved . . .'. The opening phrase was used again in the Chapter House at York. Carved roses appear in the voussoirs of the north transept. The first text of the *Roman de la Rose* was written about 1250. Among the miscellaneous tiles are a hunting scene and St Edward and the Pilgrim, as well as 'a quatrefoil with square sides', which is peculiar to the Westminster kiln.

The Bells

Matthew Paris' drawing of Westminster Abbey as a box to put bells in with a free-standing shrine to the east of it reflects the initial priorities in Henry III's mind. Eight new bells were made between 1248 and 1253 and hung in a special bell tower — the third and fourth bells were re-cast in 1539. Today the only survivor of the medieval bells is the frater bell, which used to call the brethren to meals.

Chapter Six

THE MEDIEVAL MONUMENTS AND CHANTRY CHAPELS

THE COLLECTION of medieval monuments in the Abbey is among the richest in the world. Presiding over them is the Shrine of St Edward the Confessor, the most complete of its kind surviving in a Protestant country. Most of the base is still here, and the body of the saint lies in the upper part.

THE SHRINE OF ST EDWARD

Henry III started work on the shrine in 1241, at the same time as Louis IX received from Constantinople the relic of the Crown of Thorns, which was the inspiration for the Sainte-Chapelle. In both cases the relics came first, the buildings afterwards.

Inevitably, the reliquary chest, the ultimate focus of artistic and devotional attention, no longer survives, having been destroyed at the Reformation. We can gain some idea of its appearance, from the informative drawings in the *Life of Saint Aedward*, which was rewritten probably by Matthew Paris at Henry III's insistence from the original by Aelred of Rievaulx. The chest housing the relics was of precious metal and of the usual shape, with a gabled roof, and it was flanked by statues on pillars of St Edward and the Pilgrim. The gable end included a statue of the blessing Christ flanked by censing angels, and below them the seated Edward flanked by two blessing bishops. The gable was crested with 'comma' crockets like the Retable and the St Faith wall painting, and at the apex there was a foliated finial surmounted by the Cross.

These details can be expanded by contemporary accounts of the 'basilica adorned with purest gold and precious stones'. Itself of gold, the shrine was furnished with gold images, not only of the Majesty,

Estoire de Seint Aedward le Rei, Cambridge University Library. Scene showing pilgrims before the thirteenth-century shrine.

but of five angels, of the Blessed Virgin Mary (with an emerald and a ruby), of St Peter, of St Edmund and of five kings. In addition there was an image of a king carrying a church — probably Henry III — and another of a queen bearing a flower, presented by Eleanor of Provence as early as 1236. In 1245 Edward of Westminster, who was in charge of the new Shrine works, showed the king an image of the Confessor, presumably one of the pair of the Confessor and the Pilgrim which stood on separate pillars on either side, and over the next fifteen years he sought out a cameo and precious jewels to set into the shrine. During the upheaval of the building works from 1252-3 the shrine reposed in a special chapel in the Palace of Westminster. In 1267 came Henry III's political nadir, when he had to pledge the gold images of the shrine — valued at £2,555 — to meet his necessities, but by 1269 the shrine had been made good for the great Translation.

Edward of Westminster had died in 1264, so the refurbishing was in the hands of William of Gloucester, the most important practising goldsmith in Henry III's employ and the designer of the second Great Seal of Henry III issued in 1259, with finials and cresting of the same type as those on the shrine gable. On 13 October 1269 Henry III, his brother Richard Earl of Cornwall and his two sons carried the shrine to its new place of honour on a lofty stone base behind the High Altar 'on high like a candle upon a candlestick, so that all who enter into the House of the Lord may behold its light'. Henry gave to the adornment of the shrine the relic of the stone with the marks of Christ's feet from his Ascension, a relic of the girdle of the Virgin and four silver basins for lamps. Edward I subsequently gave it the Crown of Llewellyn and the spoils of his Scottish victory, and from 1290 there were three great candlesticks. Richard II gave it a costly silver table enamelled with the story of the Confessor and the Pilgrim, while Caxton saw here an impression of King Arthur's Seal set in beryl.

The Shrine of the Confessor was the heart of royalty, until it was raided in July 1536 on the orders of Thomas Cromwell, the shrine itself melted down and the encrusted offerings sent to Henry VIII. The body of the Confessor was reburied, probably under the dismembered stone base.

It is that base which we have still, reassembled after the iconoclasm of 1536, but not accurately. It once stood on four steps, of which one, with depressions made by innumerable knees, has been replaced back to front. The patterns of the arched headings of the three recesses either side no longer tally. The projecting cornice is an addition and the plinth below it has been extended. The inscription course below that is of the reconstruction and reads: OMNIBUS INSIGNIS VIRTUTEM LAUDIBUS: HEROS: SANCTUS EDWARDUS, CONFESSOR, REX VENERANDUS: QUINTO DIE JAN. MORIENS 1065. SUPERAETHERA: SURSUM CORDA.   I.F.

The inscription, and others like it in Roman capitals, were the work of Abbot Freckenham, who reconstructed the shrine base during the brief Catholic interlude of Queen Mary I. On 20 March 1557 the Confessor's relics were reinstated 'in ye sam plasse wher ye shryne was and ytt shalle be sett up agayne as fast as my lord Abbott can have yet don . . .'. Freckenham interred the Confessor within the enlarged platform of the original base which he had put together in four months. Beneath Freckenham's inscription a section of the original inscription was found in the eighteenth century, verifying the record of it in the history of 1460 by an Abbey monk, Richard Sporley:

1) + ANNO: MILENO: DOMINI: CUM (?) SEPTVAGENO: ET
2) BIS: CENTENO: CUM: COMPLETO: QUASI: DENO: HOC: OPVS: EST: FACTVM: QUOD: PETRVS:
3) DVXIT: IN: ACTVM: ROMANVS: CIVIS: HOMO:
4) CAVSAM: NOSCERE: SI VIS: REX: FVIT: HENRICVS: SANCTI: PRESENTIS: AMICVS.

SEPTUAGENO must surely have been a mistake for SEXAGENO as the remains of Edward the Confessor were enshrined above this base in 1269. Are we to believe that the base beneath his shrine was not completed until ten years later?

In its basic disposition, the shrine base follows a norm. The three recesses either side were to accommodate pilgrims, some of whom endeavoured to spend the night as near as possible to the remains of the saint. The central partition is only a stone's thickness, and those remains were out or reach, originally in the golden shrine and since 1557 in the upper part of the base. The half-buried twisted column at the north-west angle gives the best impression of the original glory of the base, with its mosaic, inlaid glass and precious marbles. Purbeck marblers no doubt collaborated in cutting away their slabs to take the exotic inlays. They must have cut the larger foliate capitals, but for the rest the surface was Italian work.

There are blocked holes in the high vault over the shrine through which pulleys lifted and lowered the original cover that concealed and protected the burning splendours of the shrine itself. The base has been restored slightly off its original centre — the central boss from which the apse ribs radiate should be immediately over the middle of the shrine. Its original altar served the secondary purpose of enclosing the remains of those of Henry III's children who died young, and was therefore preserved as a monument when it might no longer serve as an altar. It is now half buried in a recess in the south ambulatory, and is of Cosmati workmanship. The centre of the top is occupied, not by a piece of marble or provision for a relic recess, but by a rough and uneven stone. Among Henry III's gifts to the Shrine was the stone with the mark of Christ's footprint: if this was incorporated in the mensa it would explain Henry's preference for his children to be buried in so holy and hopeful a setting. Ill-shapen and of no metallic value, the relic — if such it is — appears to have been overlooked in 1536 and to have remained where Henry set it.

On 17 November 1558 Queen Mary died, and Freckenham's new shrine was never made. All he had achieved was an oak canopy which does something to conceal the absencce of the shrine he planned to put beneath it. The canopy is of a restrained Classicism, inlaid with blue and gold glass mosaics and has been carefully restored using a measured drawing by John Talman of 1713.

THE CONFESSOR'S CHAPEL

Henry III

Henry III decided in 1246 to be buried here, and so made the Abbey the chief mausoleum of English kings as well as the Coronation

Church. His choice of the Abbey was both a return to the precedent of Edward the Confessor, who lies here with his Queen, Edith, beside him, and a departure from the practice of his immediate forebears who, with the exception of his father John, had been buried at Fontevrault in western France — a territory lost by Henry III's time.

Henry's remains were first laid in 1272 'before the High Altar' in the place previously occupied by the Confessor. In 1274-6 the architect Robert of Beverley was paid for 300lbs of wax — enough for a full size figure fully clothed — for an image of the King, and 66s.8d. for fashioning it. The most likely position of the temporary tomb is that occupied since 1296 by Edmund Crouchback.

The most important position in the Abbey however, was not north of the High Altar but north of the Shrine of the Confessor, and Henry's permanent memorial was moved to this place. In 1280 Edward I brought precious Jasper 'de partibus gallicanis' to beautify his father's tomb. The base of the tomb, which includes the largest piece of imperial porphyry here, is of a piece with the Cosmati works of the floor, which on the sanctuary side is brought to fit it. The grille, which was made by Henry Lewis in 1290, has now disappeared. The elevation of the tomb base towards the Shrine of the Confessor is composed of a series of recesses with crosses in the back of them, once inlaid with Cosmati mosaic. All the Cosmati mosaic work within reach has been stolen.

Henry III himself recited the list of Sainted English Kings to his Historian, Matthew Paris. Henry belongs to that group, the Confessor, Henry VI, and Charles I, who are more holy than practical. Tomb bases with recesses are usually the preserve of those deceased for whom there is thought of canonization — a Westminster Chronicler of the fourteenth century tells us that miracles were expected and obtained at Henry's tomb. Whilst the Cosmati tomb of Pope Clement IV at Viterbo took a Gothic fashion in gablet architecture to Italy, the tomb base of Henry III has brought a touch of Classicism to England.

The wonderfully refined bronze effigy of Henry III, despite the loss of the two sceptres, the gables, and the lions beneath his feet, is still beautiful. It is best seen from the Chapel of St John the Baptist on the north side, and together with that of Eleanor of Castile, is the earliest surviving monument in this medium in England. It was cast by William Torel, at the same time as that of Queen Eleanor. The simple, almost abrupt folds of the drapery of Henry's effigy would have become a standing sculpture thirty years earlier, like that of the Confessor on a pillar by the Shrine. His short arms and exquisitely refined hands recall the figures on the Retable of 1268. His furrowed

LEFT: Effigy of Henry III on the north side of the shrine by William Torel 1291. RIGHT: Effigy of Eleanor of Castile by William Torel, 1291.

brow and clear cut features have many comparisons in the heads of the sculptures in the muniment room. Henry III's effigy was made by the *cire-perdu* technique. It is a very conservative work for 1291. It is probably either a literal copy or even a casting of the life-size wax temporary effigy made by Robert of Beverley in 1274-6.

The hands originally held two sceptres; Henry changed his image on the great seal of 1259 from the sword and orb to the sceptres of peace. Under the effigy on the metal base, which like his pillows is richly decorated with the lions of England, there is an incised sketch of a royal nun and another smaller nun in prayer before a damaged figure which probably represents the Virgin and Child. Henry's widow, Eleanor of Provence and her grand-daughter took the veil in 1284 at Amesbury. The message could be similar to that of Sir Otes de Grandisson praying before the Virgin on Eleanor's tomb base. The tester over the monument was originally painted.

Eleanor of Castile and Edward I

When Eleanor of Castile died in 1290, her mourning husband Edward I arranged a whole series of funereal monuments for her, which are among the most beautiful in this country. The tomb chest is of Purbeck marble, and like the Eleanor Crosses and her seal it shows shields of arms suspended from the branches of trees — the oak, the vine, the maple, the thorn, and presumably the rose. The painting on the ambulatory side of her tomb base represented four pilgrims at a sepulchre, with a knight — probably Sir Otes de Grandisson — kneeling before the statue of the Virgin. This was almost certainly painted by the king's painter Walter de Durham, along with the original wooden tester which was replaced in the fifteenth century to make way for the Chantry of Henry V. The iron grille, the most elaborate of its date surviving, was made by Thomas of Leighton for £12 plus 20s. for carriage in 1294, and still carries prickets, provision for candles which were to burn here day and night, for two hundred and fifty years. In 1291 William Torel was paid £113.6s.9d. for three gilt bronze memorials of the Queen: this effigy; one to go over her entrails at Lincoln Cathedral; and one over her heart in the Blackfriars Church in London. (The royal confessors were Dominican.)

Eleanor's cushions and slab are ornamented in a fabric pattern with the lions of Leon and the castles of Castile. It was said at the time that sculptors make their figures of the Blessed Virgin Mary in her likeness. She wears her hair long and flowing. The little indentations around the hem of her robe and along the strap of her mantle once contained precious or semi-precious stones, which also ornamented her crown. She has lost the supporters beneath her feet.

Her husband Edward I occupies the last surviving space on the north side of the Shrine, but with no effigy. According to Langtoft's contemporary Chronicle he was buried here 'in Toumbe de Marbre Ben Polye'. On great occasions the tomb chest was covered in a great cloth of gold, and it may have been used as an Easter Sepulchre. The glory of the monument was the canopy above it, which is sadly lost.

Edward III and Philippa of Hainault

John Orchard was probably the artist of the effigy of Edward I's grandson Edward III, as well as that of the Black Prince at Canterbury. Both effigies represent the finest English craftsmanship of their time — good, solid work, if a trifle dull. Edward bears two sceptres. The alternation of the Royal Arms quartering his claim to France with the arms of St George along the base are in keeping with the nature of his reign.

The fourteen children of Edward III, alive or dead, formed the weepers around his tomb. Those on the ambulatory side are still there and represent, from left to right, the Black Prince; Joan de la Tour; Lionel Duke of Clarence; Edmund Duke of York; Mary Duchess of Brittany; and William of Hatfield. Lionel Duke of Clarence is almost

The effigy of Edward III (d. 1377) by John Orchard.

a miniature copy of his father, and the face and beard of the Black Prince are very similar again.

Edward III's effigy is regarded as the first English example of portraiture: the gilt bronze resembles the wooden funereal effigy head which is the earliest we have. Edward sustained a stroke three days before his death: the mouth of the wooden head is drawn down to one side, a probably result of the stroke. Stephen Hadley was paid £22.4s.11d. for an 'image in the likeness of a king' for the funeral. In his gilt bronze Orchard has glossed over the distorted mouth, but otherwise copied the funeral image.

Edward III still has five angels within the shafts that supported his canopy. The base of his tomb was almost certainly designed by Henry Yeveley — compare the bases of Cardinal Langham and Richard II, for which he was certainly responsible. These all represent a retreat from the new articulation of Philippa's tomb base in favour of the traditional flat patterning with much provision for shields of arms. The tester is a new departure, with an entirely architectural treatment, similar to Yeveley's canopy work of the Chantry of John of Gaunt, made between 1369 and 1374 and formerly in St Paul's Cathedral. The effigy gazes at an intricate and delicate vault, designed by Hugh Herland, Master Carpenter to Edward III and Richard II, rather than at a Holy Image. By 1377, when Herland, Yeveley and Wynford were at the height of their powers, architecture was the pre-eminent artistic form in England.

The monument to Edward III's queen, Philippa of Hainault, breaks the sequence of gilt bronze effigies round the Shrine. Edward III spent approximately £300 on this monument, among the most costly in the Abbey. Sadly it has been much mutilated, but a hundred years ago gold patterns, coloured jewels and beads were still visible on the black and white marble. A century earlier the engraving on her crown could be seen. In 1850 two of her weepers and an angel were found buried in the staircase turret of Henry V's Chantry — only one weeper remains unstolen. The effigy was carried out by Jean de Liege in 1367, two years before Philippa's death. The miniature tomb for Philippa's long dead children in the Chapel of St Edmund and the six angels of her own tomb, were made by John Orchard in 1376. The surviving angel had wings of gilt metal.

One of the special features of this effigy must have been her hands carved free from the block of her body, and now, therefore, inevitably lost. Understatement may be the keynote of the lumpy effigy of a woman of fifty-five, but it was supported by over seventy statuettes, in the niches, and around what was obviously an enormously elaborate openwork housing: a piquant contrast between

Effigies of Richard II (d. 1399) and his Queen, Anne, on the south side of the shrine made upon her death in 1394.

filigree architectural setting and naturalistic figures. The openings of the niches over the Queen's head are filled with blue glass. Her tester, which has been damaged to accommodate the Chantry of Henry V, may be by Hugh Herland, since its pierced spandrels are similar to those of the Abbot's Hall, built about 1375.

Richard II and Anne of Bohemia

The monument to Richard II and his wife Anne of Bohemia was started in 1395, a year after Anne's death. Nicholas Broker and Godfrey Prest of Wood Street contracted to make two gilt images holding one another's right hands, with 'Gablitz' or 'hovels' over their heads. He was to have two lions beneath his feet, she an eagle and an leopard. In addition there were to be twelve gilt metal images of saints, whom the King would name, and eight angels round the tomb. There were to be engraved 'escriptures' and enamelled shields, and the whole monument was to be completed in two years at a cost of £400. The base of marble was commissioned from Henry Yeveley and Stephen Lote, to resemble that of Edward III.

In an eighteenth-century engraving we can see the Queen's eagle supporter. The cushions had gone and were subsequently replaced at the behest of Queen Victoria. Richard and Anne's clothes are richly engraved with the letters A and R crowned with badges of the broom pod *(Planta Genesta* = Plantagent) a tree-stock, a sunburst, and a chained and couched hart. Anne wears the crowned initials, knots and chained ostriches, collared and holding nails, and the buttons down her bodice were of precious gems. The gablet over Richard's head is engraved on its vault with the arms of the Confessor impaling France and England with chained harts as supporters; Anne's gablet has France and England quarterly impaling Bohemia with eagle supporters. Their arms are missing. They were holding hands.

On the tester ghosts of the paintings by John Hardy survive: the Coronation of the Virgin, Christ in Majesty, and Angels with shields. Both heads are convincing likenesses of real people — and yet they are strangely alike: they ought to have been brother and sister. On the other hand, Anne's face is unlike the smooth oval of her wooden funereal effigy, which is itself so generalized a face that we may suspect it was not a serious attempt at a portrait.

The drapery, by Broker and Prest, curves inwards around the feet in an Italianate style. The images of twelve saints probably took the place of weepers. Unlike Edward III, Richard had no heir and saints might have served him better than relatives. In this choice the monument echoes that to Philip the Bold by Claus Sluter and Nicholas de Werve at Dijon with mourning Carthusian monks instead of family weepers. To make way for this monument, William de Valence was ousted to St Edmunds Chapel.

Princess Margaret

Edward IV's sixth daughter Margaret died in 1472 at nine months. Her tomb of grey marble was designed to slot into the four steps on the north side of the Shrine and nestle, like thirteenth-century royal babies, against the Shrine of the Confessor.

THE CHANTRY CHAPEL OF HENRY V

In his Will, made in 1415, Henry V had specified a high chantry chapel over his tomb. The contrivance whereby his wishes were met has done more to alter the original design of the Abbey from the inside than any other feature. In detail and near to, the ingenuity and fascination of Henry V's Chantry forgives it quite, but at a distance the distortion of the two central pillars of the apse is hard to excuse.

In the event the altar of the relics was moved to block the way between Henry III's monument and the shrine. Encroachments were made on the monuments of Queens Eleanor and Philippa in order that a bridge might spring from the Confessor's Chapel across the ambulatory, with Henry V's Chantry Chapel upon it.

The memorial to Henry V was made in two stages: the tomb itself, and the chantry chapel over it. Initially, his Purbeck marble tomb was situated beside the then surviving altar of the Trinity on the platform specially extended into the ambulatory. The present modern bridge provides an opportunity to study this tomb chest, designed as were those to the south west of it by Yeveley; but this one has recesses. Henry V was another candidate for sainthood.

Only the wooden core remains of Henry V's silvered and gilt effigy, once the most splendid in the Abbey. The head, hands and regalia were all of solid metal. The lions and antelope from beneath his feet, the angels arranging his pillow, the orb with its crown and the sceptre and two gold teeth were stolen before 1467. In January 1545 the head with its gilt crown and hands and the rest of the silver plating were taken. The present head and hands were built up of fibre glass by Louisa Bolt in 1971. The head was based on the portrait in the royal collection and the figure was given an orb and sceptre. The effigy of Henry V gazes, like that of Edward III, not at a painted tester but at an elaborate vault, the eastern bay of which has a central boss of the hollow crown — the heavenly crown for which Henry had exchanged his earthly one.

The chantry chapel, which this double vault supports, was undertaken in 1437. The most striking feature of this bold structure is the pair of turrets containing spiral staircases which are simultaneously the hollow eastern piers which support the upper stage. Statues mount the hollow spirals, as they had mounted an open staircase designed by Jean of Liege in the Louvre in 1365. This deft design resembles a miniature gatehouse, and was the masterpiece of John Thirsk, Master Mason of the Abbey from 1420 until his death in 1452. Over the 'gateway' a low register accommodated a pair of seated figures in the centre, no doubt Saints Peter and Paul with a miniature (surviving) statue of the Virgin above them, and four seated ladies on either side, probably the four Cardinal Virtues. The lowest pair of figures against the spiral staircases are bishops or mitred abbots. Above them two kings carry buildings — probably Henry III and Sebert as founders of the Abbey. Above the two doors are the Confessor and the Pilgrim, then St Catherine (Henry's Queen's name saint) on the north, St Edmund on the south, and above them cardinals. The last pair are James the Great and John the Evangelist.

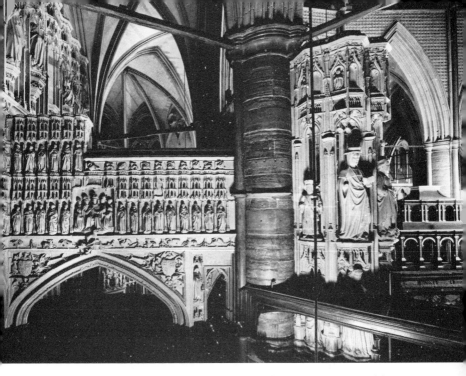

The north face of the chantry bridge of Henry V by John Thirsk, 1437-41. The reredos of the bridge chapel and the shrine of the Confessor are visible.

The two coronations on the flanks of the bridge surely represent Henry V's two thrones as King of England and Regent of France. The two images of him on horseback with fortified cities behind him have been interpreted as the King jumping a stream, but surely for 'stream' we should read the English Channel. Among the liberal armorial devices, Henry V's antelope and horse mill represent his motto 'After busie labour cometh victorious reste'.

Within the chantry chapel itself the reredos expresses the Dedication to the Trinity, to the Annunciation, and to All Saints, here typified by Edward the Confessor and Edmund, George and Denis, Patron Saints of England and France. The frieze below this reredos has an inscription of which the word 'requiem' survives, and three trefoils with reliefs. The centre trefoil had a cross and sword with light radiating from it, and the others are the Virgin and Child with light streaming from them, seated on the moon, and the Virgin and Unicorn. Apocalyptic commentaries foreseeing the third age of the Spirit were part of the highly personal mystical literature of the 'Devotio Moderna' the religious awakening in which Henry had a considerable interest.

The original grilles enclosing Henry V's tomb were by Roger

Johnson, who was paid for the work on 28 January 1431. These were taken down again and sold in 1441 as part of the construction of the chantry chapel, so the present iron grating, reinstated along with that of Eleanor of Castile's by Scott, dates from the completion in about 1451. An arrow found in the staircase turret has been assumed to belong to the armaments brought into the Abbey in 1554. It is more likely to have fallen from the beam carrying Henry's accoutrements of war: his helmet, saddle, and sword are now in the museum — surely he would have borne an arrow from Agincourt.

The soft limestone of the tomb has perished badly, blunting every arris and taking the surface from the sculpture. Twenty of the canopies collapsed in the late seventeenth century, and only Lethaby's limewash has kept the surface together at all.

THE AMBULATORY AND RADIATING CHAPELS

All the radiating chapels round the ambulatory contain medieval tombs of considerable interest, of which only a few can be mentioned here. Most of the chapels are peopled by the medieval aristocracy, but the clergy gathered around the Chapels of the two SS John with between them.

Chantry Chapel of Abbot John Islip

All that remains of the enrichment of Abbot Islip's (d. 1532) double chantry chapel are two grisaille paintings of kings and the marble slab and columns of fluted bronze and acanthus capitals now forming an altar in the upper chapel; and in the lower chapel a broken bust of the blessing Christ in the eastern window recess, and the lower part of a roundel which once held a bust of Christ on the western exterior. This bust may now be in the Wallace Collection.

The obituary roll commemorating Islip's death gives us an idea of what both the High Altar and the chantry chapel looked like. It is illustrated by exquisite line drawings, probably by Gerard Horenbolte, who also ornamented Patent Rolls 1526-29. The drawing of Islip's hearse before the High Altar shows that High Altar and the angels on the brackets of Crouchback's monument whilst the drawing of the chantry chapel affords an almost complete account of its original appearance. The eastern wall of the upper chapel was edged with a band of angels in quatrefoils, perhaps part of the thirteenth-century work, framing a painting of the Last Judgement and a Crucifixion. The same subject in the lower chapel stood below an Assumption, and the structure of Islip's monument was made up of

LEFT: Joan de la Tour, a daughter of Edward III from the base of his tomb by John Orchard, 1377. RIGHT: Heads of alabaster effigies of Baron Daubeny (d. 1508) and his widow, Elizabeth, in the Chapel of St John the Baptist.

the features now forming the upper altar. The frieze of saints outside the chapel and shields bearing the arms of the Passion are legible in the drawing.

To the east of this chantry chapel is the framework of an altar piece of St Erasmus from his Chapel built by Queen Elizabeth Woodville and displaced during the demolition of the east end of the Abbey. Abbot Islip reinstated it in a niche ornamented with his rebus — a pun on his name using an eye for 'I' and a slip or branch, also found on his chantry chapel.

Our Lady of the Pew

The 'secret' Chapel of Our Lady of the Pew can be dated to the later fourteenth century by the two pert little angels acting as stops to the severely rectangular moulding around its entrance arch, bearing the arms of St Edward the Confessor and of England quartered with France ancient. It is possible that this chapel was created out of the solid pier in response to the bequests of Mary of St Paul (d. 1377), widow of Aymer de Valence. In which case the silhouette of a standing figure with rays radiating from its head within the recess in the north wall originally contained her alabaster statue of the Virgin. The

Weepers from the tomb of John of Eltham (d. 1334).

central boss still has its carving of the Assumption of the Virgin, whilst other bosses are ornamented with roses and angel heads. The vault of the inner bay on the west side comes down on two head corbels, an old king and a young king — surely Edward III and Richard II. The chantry chapel is richly decorated with polychrome patterns throughout, though the badge of Richard II — a White Hart gorged — which was visible on the east wall fifty years ago may have perished. The statue in the northern niche is a modern alabaster.

The Chapels of St John the Baptist and St Paul

In the Chapel of St John the Baptist is the little altar tomb to Hugh and Mary de Bohun. Made of Purbeck marble between 1260 and 70, this tomb was used 'second hand' for the children now within it, surely a result of Henry III's and Edward I's decision to inter royal babies within the altar of the Shrine of the Confessor.

The screen monument to Sir Louis Robessart, Henry V's standard bearer, divides the Chapel of St Paul from the ambulatory. It is splendidly heraldic, featuring his crest of a sultan's head surrounded by a Catherine wheel, but was sadly repainted during the 1960s. Inside the chapel is the monument to Giles Daubeny, first Baron Daubeny, and his widow Elizabeth. Only the pair of alabaster effigies are original, and these were repainted when the monument was refurbished and the grille added in 1889. Observe their blunted shoes, and beneath his the pair of bedesmen.

The Chapel of St Edmund

Vandalism of the exquisite thirteenth-century wall arcading apparently started before 1400 when the monument to Sir Bernard Brocas with his head propped on a tilting helmet with its Moors Head crest and his feet on a lion was driven into the wall. Both the monument and its lean and pretty late fourteenth-century canopy were refurbished and repainted in the eighteenth century.

The alabaster tomb of John of Eltham, also in the Chapel of St Edmund, is one of the first masterpieces of the Nottingham alabasterers. The weepers, among the most exaggerated and delicious little figurines of the fourteenth century, are set against a foil of black touch. The craftsmen and their patrons were aware of the value of this translucent material against a dark background — the effect is comparable with Jean Pucelle's illuminations or the penmanship of the Masters of Queen Mary's Psalter — that of a cameo. Details of hems, belts and other items were picked out in colour. The best weepers are the pair against the ambulatory, where nobody has knocked off or stolen the heads. They appear to be dancing a minuet. The canopy of this tomb was of delicate wrought spires and masons' work intermixed and adorned with little images and angels. What a loss.

Of thirty-five recorded medieval tombs from the Limoges workshop, the most important of the five survivors is the monument to William de Valence (d. 1296). William, with his family connections with Lusignon, expressed in the shields of de Lusignon, Pembroke and Lacey still visible on the tomb, had personal associations with the Limoges area. This tomb was made of eighty pieces of Limoges enamelling which are screwed onto a wooden base. Only a small proportion of these survive, of which the most substantial is his shield. The damaged oak base shows scratched shields of arms for placing the enamelled ones. The curiously asexual and archaic features of de Valence are almost identical with a funerary mask of Limoges workmanship in the Cluny Museum in Paris. This tomb was probably displaced by Richard II.

The Chapel of St Benedict

In the Chapel of St Benedict is the monument to Cardinal Simon Langham (d. 1376). The tomb chest is by Henry Yeveley and Stephen Lote, whilst the effigy is of alabaster with inlays of blue glass and originally had coats of arms painted on it. The medieval grille survives, though the canopy was destroyed in the eighteenth century. Langham presides over the Chapel wearing his mitre as Archbishop of Canterbury rather than his Cardinal's hat.

THE SANCTUARY

Edmund Crouchback and Aveline of Lancaster

The most splendid of the trio of monuments on the north side of the sanctuary is that to Edmund Crouchback, Earl of Lancaster (d. 1296). This has been attributed to Michael of Canterbury, chief architect of the court around 1300. It is made of Reigate stone and completely covered with painting (in a linseed oil medium). The framework is gold with red and blue, and silver is used under glazing on the vaults. The monument deserves loving examination, from the foliate designs over a miniature vault to the tiny dots on the stubble of one of the weeper's beards. Edmund himself wears a striped coat, possibly of exotic origin, and in the apex of the canopy on both sides he is depicted seated upon his horse praying towards the high altar. The monument is studded with imitation glass jewels.

The effigy leans towards the high altar in a gesture of prayer, an Italian idea, and was probably carried out by Master Alexander of Abingdon. The mourners at his funeral, each identified by a shield of arms, are lively figurines. The subtlety of painted glazes, and the decoration of slender pilasters with painted tracery and masonry patterns blur the edges between the arts.

Edmund's wife Aveline, Countess of Lancaster, died in 1273 at the age of 14. Her husband almost immediately remarried, so that the provision of an elaborate tomb for her twenty years after her death is very improbable. Her monument follows the disposition of a ciborium tomb against a wall, the models being the tombs at Royaumont of Blanche and Jean de France, children of St Louis, who died in 1243 and 1247. Their recesses were occupied by paintings of the standing figures of the dead within painted canopies. According to Lethaby, a little trefoil in the gable of Aveline's tomb carried the painted figure of Aveline transported by angels to heaven. A further painted trefoil is still visible at the apex of the gable on the ambulatory side.

The effigies of Aveline and her weepers are of exquisite grace. The critical dating feature of Aveline's monument is the crockets along the canopy, which are of a type not usually found before the 1290s. The tomb appears to be the earliest of the 'ciborium' type in England.

Effigy of Edmund Crouchback, (d. 1296).

Aymer de Valence

The monument between Aveline and her husband, Edmund Crouchback is to Aymer de Valence, Earl of Pembroke (d. 1324). It makes no improvements upon that of Edmund Crouchback. The arches have taken on the acutely pointed ogee, and there is more reliance upon foliate detail than tracery. Within the trefoil in the apex of the canopy, where Edmund Crouchback prayed upon his ambling horse, de Valence gallops. Where Crouchback had two angel brackets either side of his canopy, Aymer de Valence has three. His weepers however wear simpler swinging draperies which emphasize their graceful poses. His legs are crossed, as are those of Edmund, not to indicate the Crusades, but the alertness of the Solider of Christ.

THE BRASSES

There are relatively few brasses in the Abbey — even in the Middle Ages their use would have been a discreet solution to the problems of over-crowding. The brass crosses laid into the de Valence slabs under the tomb of Henry V are among the earliest surviving brasses in the country. Brasses were chosen by three figures of some importance in the late fourteenth century: Robert Waldby, Archbishop of York (1397), John of Walton, Bishop of Salisbury (1395) (not visible); and

Eleanor, Duchess of Gloucester (1399). Both Robert Waldby and Eleanor Duchess of Gloucester in St Edmund's Chapel are fine examples of the English system of the silhouette brass with silhouette canopy. Among the abbots only John Estney (d. 1498), now in the ambulatory, chose this format.

HENRY VII'S CHAPEL

The Sculptural Decoration in the Chapel

The statues outside Henry VII's Chapel represented the Apostles, Patriarchs and Kings of Judah. The prodigious array within was given over to the fullest muster of saints surviving from the late English Middle Ages. The company assembled round the image of Christ in the central niche of the east wall, and the precious image of the Virgin which Henry bequeathed for the main altar — Henry VII's Chapel retained the dedication to Our Lady. There was provision for one hundred and nine figures. The larger ones are on opposite walls of the five radiating chapels, and formed reredoses at the east end of both aisles. The smaller ones, sixty-nine in total, occupy a single row between the arcade and the clearstorey, interrupted only by the nominal chancel arch, on which are stacked the four Doctors of the Church (one missing) in pairs opposite the four Evangelists.

There are few difficulties of identification, except in the western bay, where ten lively figures consulting books and scrolls have been called Philosophers, but may be Prophets — Prophets always wear the best hats. The figures from the central niches of the larger groups in the chapel are all missing, presumably forcibly removed by the Reformers. The south aisle was intended from 1505 as a chantry for Margaret Beaufort: between St Catherine and St Margaret was presumably the Blessed Virgin Mary. The north aisle may have been intended for Henry VII's heirs: here is St Armagilus of Ploërmel in Brittany, reputed to have been Welsh or Cornish, and a dragon tamer, peculiarly qualified to have received Henry's prayers when in exile. Opposite him is St Laurence with his gridiron. The figure between them may be Henry VI, who has also been suggested for the blank niche in the axial chapel, where 'HR' appears on the pedestal. However, Thomas Becket ought to have stood there, between Denys and Paul.

The Reformers spared the presiding row to the east, where the blessing Christ with his foot of the orb is flanked by the Annunciation, repeating the iconography of the altar wall of Henry V's Chantry. Beyond them are St Peter and St Paul, and the remaining Apostles.

St Sebastian and his tormentors from an apsidal chapel of Henry VII's Chapel.

Connoisseurs will enjoy St Anne teaching the Virgin to read and scep-
tics may pay their devotions to the bearded lady St Wilgefort. A few
saints are repeated: Roche who specialised in the plague; Edward the
Confessor; Laurence; and Margaret. Choice for one of the altar walls

135

Effigies of Henry VII and Elizabeth of York made by Pietro Torrigiano from 1572.

did not disqualify from the general assembly — Sebastian twice gained three niches for himself and two archers.

This ambitious programme makes visible the statement in Henry VII's Will: 'I trust also to the singular mediations and prayers of all the holy company of heaven: that is to say, Angels, Archangels, Patriarchs, Prophets, Apostles, Evangelists, Martyrs, Confessors and Virgins, and especially to mine accustomed Avouries I call and cry . . .'. Angels are here in force, supporting the Tudor and Beaufort arms with which the chapel is peppered. Nor does the chapel lack marginalia: a string course running at eye level under the complex oriel windows of both aisles is peopled with little grotesques. The sculptor in charge was probably Laurence Ymber, who carved Elizabeth of York's funerary effigy.

The Funerary Monuments

The original idea for the disposition of monuments within Henry VII's Chapel was quite different from what we see today. Henry VII planned for himself a black and white marble tomb with bronze statues and kneeling effigies in a 'closure of metall in manner of a Chapell . . . before the high aulter . . .'. Behind that altar was surely the place intended for the shrine of Henry VI. An early sixteenth-century drawing, bearing a later inscription identifying it as Henry VI's tomb, is in the British Library. It shows a turretted Chantry

Chapel over a table tomb with panelled sides. Its detailing is close to that of the chapel itself.

After their death Henry VIII gave to his parents the space meant for Henry VI, hoping to have something still more splendid for himself in the centre of the chapel. The sculptor Pietro Torrigiano had been commissioned by Prior Bolton to make a monument for Henry VII's mother, Lady Margaret Beaufort, and was subsequently contracted for a further monument for Henry VII and Elizabeth of York in 1512. The work was to be completed in six years at a cost of £1,500. Henry VIII ordered one for himself at the same time, at a cost of £2,000, but this was never made.

Torrigiano brought to the recumbent effigies of Henry VII and Elizabeth of York his gifts for idealized portraiture and the dramatic handling of drapery. He has used the simplest gesture of prayer, with no orbs or sceptres — there were no kings in Florence or Rome. His prototype was probably the tomb of Pope Sixtus IV in St Peter's, Rome, finished in 1493 by the Pollaiouli. Torrigiano had never seen his sitters: he used 'patrons' painted from living likenesses by Meynnart Venwicke, and may also have worked from wooden effigies, which still survive. When comparing the gilt bronzes with these wooden effigies, discount Henry's wooden nose, which was lost in the Second World War and replaced from Torrigiano's effigy.

Other than in replacing kneeling effigies with recumbent figures, Torrigiano kept to the letter of Henry VII's Will. The twelve saints in Renaissance roundels of olive branches, with Tudor emblems in the spandrels, are Henry VII's ten 'avouries' with the Virgin and St Christopher to make up the number. He has disposed them in dialogue, like the pairs by Donatello on the doors of the sacristy of San Lorenzo in Florence. The dramatic device points up the juxtapositions. With what urgent message is the Confessor interrupting St Vincent? It appears St Anne does not want to be introduced to St Christopher. St George stands in the pose of Donatello's statue outside Or San Michele. The angels carrying armorial bearings have become bambini, and their standards have gone.

The effigies are of dignity, restraint and intelligence. Torrigiano's masterpiece is much concealed by 'the closure of copper and gilt' that Thomas the Ducheman was working on already in 1505. This resembles a miniature chapel, with angle turrets and two stories of windows, in which heraldic emblems frequently take the place of tracery. In the centre of each side is a candle bracket with a drip pan or crown resting on a Tudor rose. Figures were stolen from the screen in 1579 and it was despoiled by the Cromwellians in 1643. The gilt has gone, but six figures of saints remain in position, but for a hand or two:

LEFT: Cherub supporting shield of arms from the base of the tomb of Henry VII and Elizabeth by Pietro Torrigiano. RIGHT: Effigy of Margaret Beaufort, d. 1509, by Pietro Torrigiano in the south aisle of Henry VII's Chapel.

James the Great, John the Evangelist, Edward the Confessor, Bartholomew, George and another. The chantry altar, for which there is scant room within the 'closure' was dedicated to the Saviour.

Torrigiano's contribution to both the Abbey and to English sculpture is most readily understood by studying the effigy of Lady Margaret Beaufort. Like those of Henry VII and Elizabeth of York, it is of gilt bronze and originally had coloured flesh. This convincing image of a shrewd and learned lady, foundress of Oxbridge colleges, was probably also based on a 'patron' by Meynnart Venwicke, who painted her towards the end of her life. Torrigiano did not reach England until 1511, two years after her death. Her feet rest on her supporter, the fabled Yale, which has lost its single horn. The screen was not added until 1526.

The Furnishings

The chapel altarpiece was carefully reconstructed by Sir W. Tapper in 1935, following the appearance of the original of 1520 as shown in old engravings. The pillars and some small sections of the marble freize are authentic. The design was probably by Torrigiano, and the carving by Benedetto da Rovezzano. The painting of the Virgin and Child above the altar is by the mid-fifteenth-century Venetian artist Bartolemeo Vivarini.

The Benedictine monks said the Offices of Our Lady in the old Lady Chapel, and to continue that purpose the western end of Henry VII's Chapel was furnished with stalls like a collegiate chapel. The back row of the three western bays, with their returns, and the steps with 'flying buttresses' and heraldic beats climbing them, plus the statuette of a king, are original. The fourth bay to the east was extended c. 1725 to accommodate the Knights of the Bath.

The original canopies were so lavish that they were continued round to the back, which was fortunate, as c. 1725 spare canopy backs were spliced off and brought round for the eastern bay. Their shafts are 1820. The front row of stalls are 1832.

The misericords deserve study. Those of 1725 and 1832 are disarming. Of the original ones, at least three deal with the snares of love; there are a number of babewyns or monkey tricks, and several figures from Aesop. Many deal with dragons, and two at the west end show monks carried off by devils. One of the most important, with the supporters carved as well as the centre, is the Judgement of Solomon, a subject Henry VIII took to himself. The two return stalls have vine harvest subjects. In the second bay of the south range is a thirteenth-century misericord carved with stiff leaf foliage. Another, evidently from the same series, is in the Museum. It has been suggested that these came from the choir stalls in the main body of the church, begun in 1253 under Jacob the Joiner. It is more likely that they came from the stalls of the previous Lady Chapel, in which case they are the earliest surviving misericords in England.

The pulpit now in the nave was presumably part of the original furnishings of Henry VII's Chapel. It retains its sounding board, a rare survival at this date, and exhibits the typically Tudor motif of linenfold panelling, also found in the Jericho parlour which was furnished before 1530. The relatively numerous pulpits surviving from the fifteenth century onwards reflect the growing popularity of sermons in the vernacular.

The vast array of medieval heraldic glass in the west window of Henry VII's Chapel was almost totally destroyed in the 1939-45 War — a record of what it looked like can be found in the photographs in the Royal Commission on Historical Monuments Volume of 1925. Panels of quarries containing Tudor emblems and 'HR's survive in the west windows of both aisles of Henry VII's Chapel, and rather mysteriously further panels, including the emblem of the crown in a rose bush, are now in the Victoria and Albert Museum. In his Will

The original bronze gates of Henry VII's Chapel, mounted on wood and ornamented with Tudor badges.

Henry VII asked that his chapel be 'glazed with stories, images, arms, badges and connissants as is by us readily devised and in Picture delivered to the Prior of St Bartholomew (William Bolton), Master of the Works'. The contract for King's College, Cambridge, itemizes windows 'after the form, manner, goodness, curiosity and cleanness of the King's new chapel at Westminster, after such manner as one Bernard Flower Glazier, lately deceased, stood to do . . .'.

Chapter Seven

THE LATER
MONUMENTS AND
THEIR SCULPTURE

THE MONUMENTS

By THE LATER NINETEENTH CENTURY the Abbey
had, it was admitted by all, become full, and although many of the
people commemorated were in their time well-known, an equally
large number was not. How then, had this come about, and what had
been, or was to be, done?

Chaucer had been buried in 1400, not as a poet, but because, not
only did he live nearby, and had held office under Richard II, but his
wife Philippa was the sister of Catherine Swynford, mistress and later
wife of John of Gaunt. He was given a monument in the south
transept by Nicholas Brigham in 1556, in recognition of his fame as a
poet.

By the time Elizabeth I ascended the throne in 1558, the church had
been stripped of altars in the various chapels which became
redundant. Those radiating round the Confessor's Chapel at the east
end soon became used as mortuary chapels and were filled with the
monuments of the Queen's relatives and members of her court. In the
chapel of St John the Baptist is one of the largest of any period, for
instance, to Elizabeth's first cousin and Lord Chamberlain, Henry
Carey, Lord Hunsdon, who died in 1596.

Change, however, was gradually coming about, for at the end of
the sixteenth century, Edmund Spenser was buried in the south
transept, the first poet expressly to be so honoured; he was followed
by others, including Ben Jonson (1637) in the north nave aisle,
although a monument to him was not erected in what was becoming
known as Poets' Corner in the south transept, until nearly a century
later. The first monument to appear on the walls west of the transepts
was in the reign of Charles I, to Mrs Jane Hill, who died in 1631, and

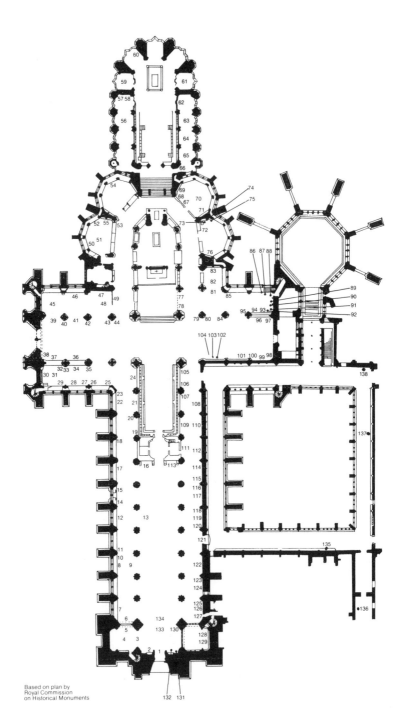

Based on plan by
Royal Commission
on Historical Monuments

142

whose claim to fame, apparently, was simply that her son was a gentleman-in-waiting to both Charles I and his father, James I.

Royal burials had continued, but now they were in Henry VII's chapel. James I commissioned monuments to Elizabeth I, and to his mother Mary Queen of Scots, whose remains were brought from Peterborough Cathedral to the chapel. A huge monument to a Stuart cousin, Ludovic, Duke of Richmond and Lennox, completely filled a chapel on the south side, but Charles I sanctioned the first non-royal burial there for his friend, George Villiers, Duke of Buckingham, murdered in 1628, and an equally splendid and large memorial swamped a corresponding chapel on the north side.

It seems to have been Oliver Cromwell who really began the use of the church as a place of burial and commemoration for national achievement — at that time, martial. The body of his son-in-law, General Ireton, was brought from Ireland to Henry VII's chapel, but when Admiral Blake was buried there in 1657, it was said that he had been laid among kings 'to encourage his officers to venture their lives'. Following the Restoration of the Stuart monarchy, however, the bodies of most of the Commonwealth leaders were ordered by Charles II to be removed as being 'unwarrantably buried since the year 1641', and many monuments were destroyed. That of Ireton, by William Wright, a sculptor of Charing Cross, had cost as much as £120. Cromwell, Ireton and Bradshaw were disinterred and hanged at Tyburn, their heads afterwards exhibited on poles at Westminster Hall. Twenty other bodies were disinterred and deposited in a pit dug in 1661 outside the north nave aisle, and to the west of St Margaret's Church.

The next few decades saw a dramatic increase in burials and the erection of monuments, and the dean and chapter had every excuse for this: they needed money for the care and maintenance of the building. Fees for interments and monuments formed a substantial proportion of the fabric fund, and these were, quite naturally, higher for the eastern parts of the church, than for the nave.

Among the first monuments erected in the nave during the late seventeenth century was that in the south aisle with its unusual bird's-eye view of a naval engagement to Sir Charles Harbord and Clement Cottrell, two young men killed when the *Royal James*, flagship of the Earl of Sandwich, was sunk by the Dutch in 1672. Harbord's father (who paid for the monument) was Surveyor-General to Charles II, while the other father, Sir Charles Cottrell, was Master 'of the Ceremonyes', so there was still connection with the court. On the other hand, the inscription on another memorial, to Major Richard Creed who was killed at Blenheim, relates that 'To his Memory his

Sorrowful Mother, Here Erects this Monument placing it near another, Which Her Son (when living) us'd to look upon with pleasure, For the worthy mention it makes of that Great man Edward Earl of Sandwich, To whom he had the Honour to be Related: And whose Heroic Virtues He was Ambitious to Imitate'. This monument was once a neighbour of that to Cottrell and Harbord, but was moved in the nineteenth century to make room for that to Major André, erected by George III.

As Dean Bradley stated at the end of the nineteenth-century, 'there was a great number [of undistinguished people] who had no claim at all, except that many of them, or their surviving friends, craved to have the honour and because there was no [local] public cemetery for those persons to be buried in . . . '. For example, James Macpherson, the reputed author of *Ossian*, so severely handled by Dr Johnson, died as far away as Inverness, but he left in his will the expression of a desire to be buried in Westminster Abbey, because he had property near. He was buried not far from Dr Johnson. Of course, if Macpherson could be brought all the way from Inverness, anyone who had property near the Abbey could be buried there . . . '.

Fabric fees for burials, established in 1717, were 'A Gent in the Body of the Church', £10; 'A Kt in the Body of ye Church', £13; 'Within any of ye Chappells', £20; a Baron, £26; an Earl, £30; a Marquess, £35; a Duke, £40; a Bishop, £30; an Archbishop, £40. In addition, an extra fee of £6 was charged for burial within the church, or £3 in the cloister.

Fees for monuments also were varied: in 1727, £31. 10 shillings was paid for the large free-standing monument to James Craggs, then in the south nave aisle, but only £21 for the memorial to Mrs Bovey, erected against the wall in the same aisle, and £10. 10 shillings in 1757 for the mural tablet to the Roman Catholic George Vertue in the west walk of the cloisters. Occasionally the dean waived the fee, as he did in 1740 when the statue of Shakespeare was put up, and any monuments which were erected by Parliament also produced no income for the fabric fund. The first of the latter was to Captain James Cornewall, who was killed at Toulon in 1744, and was so large that it blocked the arch between the nave and the south-west tower, leading into the then Consistory Court, now St George's (or the Warriors') chapel.

With almost unnoticed rapidity, the church was becoming full, not only with bodies, but also with monuments, many of which had to be accommodated on the ledge below the window. Apart from the series by Roubiliac in the south nave aisle, the one that caused the most comment, was to Admiral Tyrrell (d. 1766), of which there is now only a pathetic remnant (in the same aisle), but which once completely blocked the second window from the west. As the Admiral had, at his own request, been buried at sea, the monument was a splendidly incomprehensible assemblage of ships, rock on the sea-bed, allegorical figures and angels, with the admiral's naked body, having emerged from the water, ascending to heaven, which was represented by 'scattered masses of clouds, teeming with cherubs'. The Admiral was Irish, so the central figure at the bottom was Hibernia who, 'sitting and leaning mournfully upon a globe, points out where the Admiral's remains were deposited in the deep'. Meaningless now in its mutilated condition, and no doubt difficult to understand even when complete, nevertheless, the monument was singled out for praise by John Wesley.

Criticism and alarm at the number of monuments, as well as their destruction of the fabric, first voiced in the mid-eighteenth century, increased in volume. Thus it was decided that memorials to those killed (including Nelson) in the wars with the French should be placed in St Paul's Cathedral. But there was still worry over the number of unknown people being commemorated in the national valhalla, though then, as now, more people were attracted to the church to see the monuments, wax figures and models of churches, than to look at the architecture, although they had to pay for the privilege. The admission charge was 3d. in 1697, and this gradually increased during the following century, until it was 9d. in 1799. The money collected went to the gentlemen of the choir, who undertook to keep the monuments clean. Early in the nineteenth century, the charge was increased to 1s. 11d., which included a 'tip' for the 'tomb-shower'. However, it was not unusual for these men to seek an extra gratuity, so the dean and chapter raised the admission fee to two shillings, and put up a notice stating that guides were not to be tipped. Parliament, however, in 1825, felt that admission to the Abbey should be free, but the dean and chapter resisted, although as a precaution, they lowered the fee to 3d. for admission to the nave and Poets' Corner and one shilling to see the royal chapels, and decided to pay the choir from their own funds.

Parliament was not willing to let the matter drop and in 1841, by which time the payment to visit the royal chapels had risen to 1s. 3d., the House of Commons set up a Select Committee on National Monuments and Works of Art to enquire into the effect of freely opening the Abbey and other national buildings.

Six 'tomb-showers' were employed at that time, with an extra one during the summer months, at wages of thirty shillings, weekly, with an extra five shillings for the 'supervisor'. This amounted to about

£416 annually, which had to be paid out of the admission fees. In addition £60 had to be found to pay one of Sir Francis Chantrey's men. Joseph Theakston, to clean each monument once a year. The tomb-showers were still not allowed to accept tips, but they were only human, as one of them related, 'I told the gentleman that I was not privileged to receive it, and then he said, "Well, then I shall leave the money there,"; and he did so. It was left on the monument, and if I had not taken it someone else would'.

Theakston's work, however, did not meet with the approval of E W Brayley (the author of a great work, published in 1818, which described every monument and gravestone), who complained that much damage had been caused by his use of sand and a scrubbing brush, and that the monument to Lord Bourchier had been 'washed over of a dingy stone colour'. The Surveyor, Edward Blore, said that the monuments were not his concern but were 'under the charge of . . . Chantrey'. Brayley also stated that the boys of Westminster School were responsible for heads missing from the monument to André and that the damage was 'said to have been purposely done'. Allan Cunningham, an assistant to Chantrey, complained, as did Brayley, of the 'great devastation' caused to monuments by the erection of stands and seats for coronations. After that of Queen Victoria, Cunningham had counted at least 24 toes, fingers and pieces of drapery that had been knocked off and 'many tender and projecting parts were broken; the toes of a beautiful figure by Westmacott were broken by a plank falling on them; other monuments were broken; among them that fine one by Flaxman to Lord Mansfield . . .'.

Brayley told the Select Committee that some damage caused by workmen had been done wantonly and, then 'In respect to the monument to Edmund Crouchback, Earl of Lancaster, I have made some remarks in the second volume of my work . . . "his monument is more complete in its design and much larger than that of Valence, yet its style and execution are very similar: like that, also, the upper part of the canopy has been most vilely mutilated. Even at the last coronation [that is, of George IV] its remaining pinnacles and finials were disgracefully taken down, for the purpose of obtaining room for a few additional seats in a temporary gallery and they are now [20 years later] lying unrestored beneath the ancient arch, over the tomb of Vaughan in the chapel of St John the Baptist. It is thus that our most elegant sepulchral monuments become progressively deteriorated and eventually destroyed, through the ill taste or negligence of those who ought to take an interest in preserving them",' and gave as his opinion that more damage had been caused in this way than by any of the Abbey's visitors.

Although no free admission was achieved immediately, when, during the 1860s the Abbey was opened during one Easter without charge, the papers were full of the praises of the well-behaved, interested and awe-struck thousands of men, women and children who had descended upon the church to see the monuments, and who had neither touched, nor caused damage.

All this publicity, of course, did nothing to solve the Abbey's problem of space, but merely gave an opportunity to anyone to air views and opinions. In May 1844, the *Ecclesiologist* wondered what could be done with the 'odious monuments' as 'worship in the presence of so many pagan nudities will clearly be next to impossible', and in 1860, the same influential journal turned its attention to the 'now revolting practice of burying in the abbey', which regarded as a sepulchral chamber was 'full to overflowing; and that no fresh interment takes place of statesman, or warrior, poet, engineer or physiologist, without the preliminary disinterment — partial or complete — of someone else. When not long since the body of Hunter was translated thither, that of an earlier genius (Ben Jonson's it was supposed), had to make way, and human remains were exhumed, the skull was handed about among bystanders, that other human remains might succeed to, or at least partake, the precarious tenancy . . . .'.

The Dean from 1864 to 1881, A P Stanley, and the architect, Sir Gilbert Scott, did their not inconsiderable best to try to find a solution. For one thing they moved, reduced, or attempted to remove altogether, some of the monuments, but in every case tried to obtain the agreement of the families concerned, not always successfully. The diary of the master-mason, Henry Poole, gives an idea of what was done. '1867. Taking down Cottington's monument, altering, reducing and refixing it . . . 1868. The monument of Dame Elizabeth Carteret (a pretty monument, 1717), next the north side of the organ, had become loose and ruinous; it was taken down and sent to Haynes, near Bedford, the residence of the then Sub-dean, who was the representative of the Carteret family', or 'that of Mrs Vincent, the wife of Dean Vincent, which by the concurrence of the representative of the family has been converted into a small quatrefoil tablet, and placed under her husband's monument'. When it was proposed to remove from a window ledge in the north nave aisle, the memorial erected by Parliament to Spencer Perceval, the only assassinated Prime Minister, and himself of royal descent through Margaret, Countess of Salisbury (the 'last Plantagenet', and mother of Cardinal Pole), the family of the Earl of Egmont objected, and nothing was done.

In February 1869, the First Commissioner of Works (nowadays, the Secretary of State for the Environment) asked the Society of Antiquaries for a list of historical tombs and monuments in the country, which might be placed under government protection. The Society decided to limit their submission to monuments to people who had died not later than 1760, and to judge them, not as works of art, but for the importance of the persons commemorated. Dean Stanley prepared a list of about a hundred in Westminster Abbey, though it was thought that 'no such protection and supervision can be needed', although 'a measure of protection must apply to the whole list of monuments deemed worthy of preservation whatever their now existing state of repair and whatever the immediate probability of their careful preservation . . . or of their liability to injury, whether from carelessness, ignorance, or malice.'

Many of the Abbey memorials were, however, under threat. During the 1850s, Sir Gilbert Scott had produced a design for an extension to the Abbey, a campo santo or funerary chapel, in order to provide additional space, a controversial idea that progressed no further at the time. However, thirty years later, the subject was again raised, only this time a Royal Commission was appointed, in 1890, and among its members were Dean Bradley, Sir Austen Layard, Sir Frederic Leighton, and Alfred Waterhouse.

The hundreds of questions asked elicited some interesting information. Although he did not produce any confirmatory evidence, the Clerk of Works estimated that at least 1,400 people had been buried within the church, and another 1,800 in the cloisters and other areas outside. There was, he thought, room for no more than 100 more inside the Abbey, provided the extensive concrete foundations were excavated, though this might affect the stability of the building. The then Surveyor, J L Pearson, thought that there would be no danger.

The Royal Commission examined several plans for additional buildings, which included a series of chapels round the chapter house, an extension from the cloisters incorporating the ruins of the former refectory, and a Monumental Chapel with a tower much higher than the Victoria Tower of the Palace of Westminster, which was to cost nearly half a million pounds, rather more than the relatively modest figure contemplated by the Commissioners.

The various witnesses pursued their own hobby-horses, aiming mainly to remove unworthy and offending monuments. This, thought Lord Leighton, would make any extension at once 'a lumber-room, something like what the French call a *salon des refusés*, for the reception of things of less value and beauty, and which are unfit to remain in such a stately edifice as the Abbey'.

It was only Archbishop Benson of Canterbury who gave an objective opinion:

'I think we must remember that the feeling about Westminster Abbey, which has begun with a religious feeling, and which has deepened with time, is associated with the fact of the monuments being there, and if you disturb the sentiment that a great man is laid to rest there for ever, you will disturb the satisfaction that is felt in placing great men there at any time. This higher effect of the monuments is very real, and on that account it is undesirable to disturb them. But also as a matter of taste I hold it undesirable. I do not think that the Abbey is so much interfered with as is sometimes said. I believe that the different styles has a great effect in drawing out the beauty of the architecture . . . Therefore, I doubt whether, though you would gain space if you took away, for instance, Lord Manfield's monument, you would gain really. You would see another arch, but that is a less advantage than you have in the different outlines. I do not know whether that is heresy'.

It was to some, and still is, but it did not matter, in the end, for the Royal Commissioners, could not agree among themselves, and nothing more was done then or since.

During the present century, few large monuments have been placed in the Abbey, but two of them are to former Prime Ministers, the Marquess of Salisbury and Sir Henry Campbell-Bannerman, but in compensation, one enormous memorial has been expelled — the first monument erected by Parliament, to Captain Cornewall, R.N., was transferred to a gloomy porch between Dean's Yard and the cloister.

To some extent, however, the fashion for monuments had faded, and was doing so during the nineteenth century in churches all over the country, as stained glass windows became considered as a more acceptable form of memorial, and the Abbey followed the trend. When interments have been allowed, for some decades they have been of cremated ashes, and the usual monument is now an inscribed floor slab.

THE SCULPTURE

Only in Westminster Abbey can one see the full range of British post-Reformation sculpture, from the sixteenth to the early twentieth century: the Abbey has become, in fact, the national gallery of sculpture. On first entering the west doors, this is exactly what it appears to be, as soon as the visitor's eyes leave the soaring lines of the nave, and roam along the walls. The monuments, having been placed in such space as was available at the time, are haphazard and in no chronological order. This must be the reason that no one yet has attempted a chronological catalogue of the sculpture which, to see in sequence, would entail hours of tramping backwards and forwards from one end of the building to the other.

This survey can do no more than to point out the most significant monuments from the immigrant sculptors of the sixteenth-century Southwark School, by way of, among others, Nicholas Stone, Francis Bird, Rysbrack, Roubiliac, Flaxman, Chantrey to Epstein. Almost every important sculptor is represented, some with over-confident masses of marble towering towards the vault, whilst others were content with more manageable and reticent works. Whatever their scale, however, it cannot be denied that the architecture has been severely affected by them. (The numbers in square brackets refer to the plan on p. 142.)

The late nineteenth-century attempts to remove many of the monuments were tempered by the universally accepted fact that hideous scars would have been left, even though the Surveyor to the Fabric in 1891, John Loughborough Pearson confidently stated that restoration of all the damage was possible. In addition, there would have been great danger of subjective selection in weeding out those sculptures considered unsuitable, for those at risk mostly dated from the eighteenth century. The attitude prevailing at the beginning of this century is adequately displayed by Francis Bond in his book on the Abbey, published in 1909. He describes the monument to Wolfe as 'execrable', dismisses those in the western aisle of the north transept as of 'comparatively little importance', and totally ignores everything by Roubiliac except for the Nightingale monument [46] which is 'the most abominable monument in the church'. In 1984, the sculpture of Roubiliac received special attention at the Victoria and Albert Museum's *Rococo* exhibition, where all his known preliminary models for monuments, including the Nightingale, were exhibited.

Although this brief survey deals only with post-Reformation monuments it is worth pointing out that Torrigiano's effigy of the Countess of Richmond [63] in Henry VII's chapel, is still essentially Gothic, and although the bronze is gilded, it was also painted in the medieval manner; a close inspection will reveal traces of pigment on the wimple and hands, and it is quite possible that the face also was once painted. As the sixteenth century progressed, the influence of the Renaissance was first apparent only in details, the earliest being on

LEFT: St Edmund's Chapel, with the monuments to the Duchess of Suffolk (d. 1559), Francis Holles (d. 1622) and Elizabeth Russell (d. 1601). RIGHT: Thomas Owen (d. 1598), detail.

the tomb-chest of the Duchess of Suffolk (d. 1559) [72], the mother of Lady Jane Grey. The effigy, still in traditional style and with stiff folds to the drapery and making concession neither to the form of the body nor gravity, lies on a well-observed and carved rush mattress. The latter was a feature of a group of immigrant sculptors who, during the second half of the century, fled to this country from the religious war in the Netherlands. Being aliens, they nearly all settled outside the City of London, in Southwark. Collectively they formed what has been called the Southwark School of tomb-makers, and virtually monopolized the market in monuments until the second decade of the seventeenth century. A large amount of their work remains in parish churches, although a great deal must have been destroyed during the Great Fire of London. The chapels round the Confessor's shrine now house the most succulent collection of them to be seen anywhere, although, unfortunately, it is not possible to identify the work of the individual workshops concerned.

Two families appear to have been the principal groups forming the Southwark School — Johnson and Cure, while a third, Colt, settled near St Bartholomew the Great, in Smithfield. They all used alabaster, colour on the effigies (most of those in the Abbey have recently been repainted), and the new Tudor aristocracy expected, and was given, lavish displays of heraldry in order to establish suitably ancient lineage, or plausible connections with medieval families, often made explicit in the inscriptions. It was quite natural that the tablet to Lady Catherine Knollys (d. 1569) [74] should mention that she was the sister of Lord Hunsdon and a first cousin of Elizabeth I, but that to the ninety-year old widow of the executed Protector Somerset [69], makes no mention of his treason, but concentrates on the fact that she was 'A Princess descended of noble lignage, being daughter of the worthie Knight Sr Edward Stanhop, by Elizabeth his wyfe, that was daughter of Sr Foulke Burgchier Lord Fitzwarin, from whome our moderne Erles of Bathe are spronge, Sonne was he unto Will'm Lord Fitzwarin, that was brother to Henry Erle of Essex and Jhon Lord Berners: Whome Will'm theire sire, sometyme Erie of Eu in Normandy, begat on Anne, the sole heire of Thomas of Woodstocke, Duke of Gloucester, younger sonne to he mighty prince Kinge Edward III, and of his wyfe Aleanoure coheire unto the tenth Humfrey de Bohun that was Erle of Hereford, Essex and Northampton, High Constable of England . . .'

Southwark effigies were usually recumbent, and often accompanied by groups of kneeling sons and daughters. In addition, there was a fairly short-lived fashion for stiffly reclining men and women, resting the chin on a hand, a pose which was, to quote a passage from the *Duchess of Malfi*, 'as if they had died of toothache', to be seen on the monuments to Thomas Owen (d. 1598) [109] and Sir Thomas Hesketh (d. 1605) [24], which, from the similarity of details, are both from the same workshop, as is another in York Minster.

Behind the effigies was often an architectural frame, decorated with strapwork, ribbons, and emblems of death, such as hour glasses, skulls, spades or scythes. The Corinthian order was favourite, and it seems that only on three monuments was the Ionic order used — Earl of Shrewsbury) (d. 1618) [76], Countess of Hertford (d. 1598) [83], and on that to Elizabeth Cecil (d. 1597) [67]. The largest monument of the period, to Lord Hunsdon (d. 1596) [52] has no effigies, but makes up for their lack with about fifty heraldic shields and obelisks decorated with military trophies.

No monument by the Johnson family has been identified, but stylistically those to Margaret, Countess of Lennox (d. 1578) [65] and William Thynne (d. 1585) [105], are from their workshop, James I commissioned the monument to Mary, Queen of Scots from Cornelius Cure and that to Elizabeth I [56] from Maximilian Colt, both fine examples of the Southwark School's free-standing

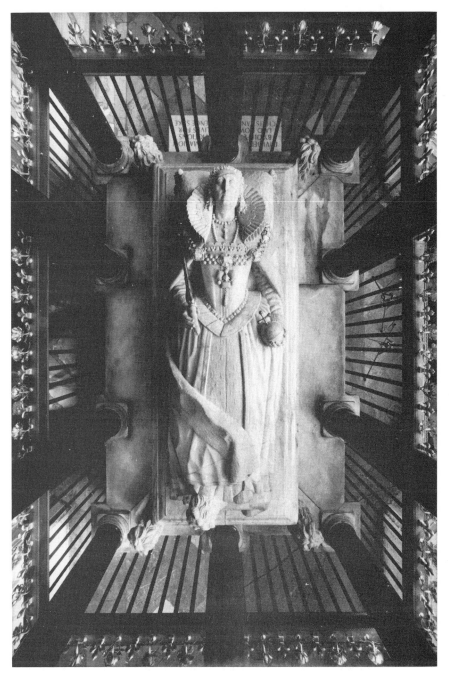

Queen Elizabeth I (d. 1603).

monuments, on which the effigy lies beneath an ornate architectural canopy. Comparison with the other Elizabethan and Jacobean monuments is instructive, because change is apparent. There is less colour and the effigies are of white marble, contrasting with the highly polished black marble elsewhere. The effigy of Elizabeth I is a portrait (unlike that of Mary, Queen of Scots [64]), which was once crowned and she wore a gilded, lead Collar of the Garter. The crown soon disappeared, but the Collar was stolen only after the railings round the tomb were removed in the 1820s. A Collar and the railings have been made recently and the crown was replaced in November 1985, but soon stolen again.

Maximilian Colt was also the sculptor of the monuments to two daughter of James I, the Princesses Sophia (d. 1600) [57] in her cradle, and Mary (d. 1607) [58]. One further sculptor is known to have provided a monument for the Abbey at the beginning of the seventeenth century, again not a native, though he had anglicized his name to Isaac James. It was that to Lord Norris (d. 1601) and his wife [45] in the Chapel of St Andrew. The effigies are still recumbent, and around them are six lively figures of sons, in armour, but on the canopy supported on eight columns, is a large superstructure with military scenes in relief on the north and south sides, the first to appear in the Abbey. The monument was once coloured and gilded, as is known from a law-suit between sculptor and painter, whose work was not considered up to standard. Unfortunately this part of the Abbey is difficult to see, as it is used as a chair store.

In the chapel of St John the Evangelist is the splendid monument to Sir Francis Vere (d. 1609) [48]. His effigy lying on a mat, on a very low plinth, is beneath a large black marble slab, supported on the shoulders of four magnificent knights in armour, though it is unfortunate that one of them is damaged, and has lost part of a leg. On the slab, is laid out the armour of the dead man. The monument is based on one of nearly a century earlier, at Breda, in Holland, and might be the work of Maximilian Colt. The figure of Elizabeth Russell (d. 1601) [75] is also something new, for she is shown seated, on a basket of osiers.

These monuments, and those to the two Queens, demonstrate that fashion was swinging away from the ostentatious and rather stereotyped form of monument (even if each is unique), which is so characteristic of the later sixteenth century. The man who led the design revolution was Nicholas Stone, the first Englishman whose work is known in some detail, through the chance survival of a notebook and an acount-book. He was an apprentice of Isaac James and, in 1606, when aged about twenty, was taken to Amsterdam by

Hendrik de Keyser, the City Architect, who was also a sculptor. Seven years later, Stone married de Keyser's daughter, and returned to England, after a valuable period absorbing new ideas, which he brought back with him.

His first monument in the Abbey, to Edmund Spenser [89], a simple white marble pedimented tablet, with volutes and swags, standing on a large base, must have been startling when put up in 1620. Equally surprising would have been the seated alabaster of eighteen-year-old Francis Holles (d. 1622) [73], and his standing uncle, Sir George Holles (d. 1626) [47], both in Roman armour, and owing some allegiance to Michelangelo's figures on the Medici tombs in Florence. Other monuments by Stone are to Sir George Villers [70] and Lord Dorchester [54], of 1631 and 1640, by which time Stone had become Master Mason to the Crown.

Contemporary with Stone's work are the huge memorials to the Duke of Richmond and Lennox (d. 1624) [61] and the Duke of Buckingham (d. 1628) [59] in Henry VII's chapel by Hubert Le Sueur. 'Sculpteur du Roi' of France, whose patron in England was Charles I. Both of these monuments, with bronze effigies, are difficult to see properly, as they are so large that they overwhelm the chapels in which they are set. The canopy over Richmond and Lennox, surmounted by Fame blowing a trumpet, is supported by life-size bronze figures of Faith, Hope, Prudence and Charity, while at the corner of Buckingham's monument sit Mars, Neptune, Pallas and Benevolence — the 'first of the host of allegorical heathenish figures which disgrace the church', in the jaundiced opinion of one Abbey historian. The Richmond and Lennox monument was repaired by order of the Earl of Darnley in 1875, as it 'had been barbarously demolished and despoiled of its metalwork, but much was left, giving authority for its restoration', according to the Abbey's Master Mason, Henry Poole.

Two monuments by Le Sueur, Lady Cottington (d. 1634) [55] and Sir Thomas Richardson (d. 1633) [106], with their busts on pedestals, were to have an impact on later monuments. Although portraiture was not normally a feature of the Southwark sculptors, they occasionally attempted it (as is apparent on one of their monuments in Canterbury Cathedral); Nicholas Stone certainly did so, and an early example by an unidentified sculptor is the bust of William Camden (d. 1623) [104]. A Master Mason after Stone (who died in 1647), was Edward Marshall, who might have worked for Stone before setting up on his own. He carved the laurel-wreathed bust of the poet Michael Drayton (d. 1631) [87], in Poets' Corner, and was probably responsible for the very fine memorial to Lionel Cranfield, Earl of

Sir George Villiers (d. 1605) by Nicholas Stone.

Middlesex (d. 1645) [82], of black and white marble, with his effigy in peer's robes lying beside his wife.

The care with which sculptors of the seventeenth century selected their materials is exhibited by the black and white marbles of Nicholas Stone's monument to Sir George Villiers and his wife, the Countess of Buckingham [70], which cost as much as £560 in 1631. The effigies lie on a splendid slab of black marble from Belgium, more than 2.1m (7ft) long and 1.5m (5ft) wide, and an equally good one of about the same dimensions is seen on the Middlesex monument.

In the chapel of St John the Baptist is another grand tomb, to Thomas Cecil, Earl of Exeter, and one of his two wives [51], although ample space was provided for his second, and surviving wife. The Earl died in 1623, aged nearly eighty, but his widow survived for another forty years and was buried in Winchester Cathedral. The sculptor is not known, but it is probable that the monument was executed during the Earl's lifetime.

Little sculpture survives from the Commonwealth; the only monument worth mentioning is that to Colonel Edward Popham (d. 1651) [50]. The somewhat ungainly standing effigies of alabaster, are probably the work of William Wright, who carved the destroyed monument to General Ireton. At the Restoration, Popham's body was ejected from the Abbey, but, exceptionally, the monument was allowed to remain provided the inscription was erased. It is often stated that the slab was simply turned round, so that the inscription is now against the wall, but Brayley noted that traces of lettering were visible on the outer face, in the early nineteenth century.

The most important sculptor of the years immediately following the Restoration was John Bushnell, who had been apprenticed to a mason-sculptor, Thomas Burman. Bushnell was forced to marry a servant seduced by Burman, and fled to the Continent, where he remained for about ten years and worked on a large monument in a Venetian church. He, therefore, had ample time to acquire first-hand knowledge of the Baroque. He was an excellent sculptor, but eventually went mad, and the effect of increasing mental instability is apparent in his work. Two simple wall monuments by Bushnell are to Sir Palmes Fairborne (114), killed in 1680 at Tangiers, and to the poet Abraham Cowley (d. 1667) [85]. The Fairborne was once flanked by obelisks bearing oval reliefs of Moorish towns, and surmounted by heads of Moors, also in relief. In St Nicholas's chapel is a memorial in the form of a pedestal, on top of which is a coronet, and at the base, four rather lumpy alabster cherub-heads, to Lady Jane Clifford (d. 1679) [68]. This is so like the pedestals that flank Bushnell's important, slightly earlier (1675) monument to Sir William Ashburnham, at Ashburnham, Sussex, that the Clifford pedestal must also be ascribed to him. The inscription is on two pieces of marble, representing parchment and which are now side by side, instead of being on opposite sides of the pedestal. It is, therefore, obvious, that the monument was at one time free-standing in the centre of the chapel, until it was squeezed against the wall in 1776, when the Northumberland vault was constructed.

A Master Sculptor to the Crown, appointed in 1684, was Grinling Gibbons, a name known to most people, but particularly for the fame attached to his skill at wood-carving. He was also a sculptor in marble, at which he was not nearly so accomplished, and none of his Abbey monuments can be considered his best work, by any means. Among the earliest of them is Mrs Mary Beaufoy (d. 1705) [11], which is lettered boldly with his name. The latest is to Admiral George Churchill (d. 1710) [112], brother to the Duke of Marlborough.

Gibbons' monument to the Duke of Newcastle (d. 1677) [41], and his second wife is old-fashioned, in that the two effigies are still recumbent, in the manner of earlier in the century. In the mid-nineteenth century, Sir Gilbert Scott wished to move the memorial, and began 'by removing from the top of the . . . monument loose and broken parts. But the Dean [Stanley] coming into the transept, dissented from the architect's views, as it would reduce the floor space of the congregation'. Gibbons' monument to Admiral Cloudesley Shovell (shipwrecked off the Scilly Isles in 1707) [108] is an ungainly, dull affair, even if it had been commissioned, as the inscription records, by Queen Anne. Between Corinthian columns, and beneath a canopy, reclines the Admiral, too large, and uninspired. Even within four years of its execution, Joseph Addison, in the *Spectator*, was complaining that the 'monument has often given me great offence instead of the brave rough English Admiral, which was the distinguishing character of that plain gallant man, he is represented on his tomb by the figure of a beau, dressed in a long periwig, and reposing himself on velvet cushions . . . The inscription is answerable to the monument; for, instead of celebrating the many remarkable actions he had performed in the service of his country, it acquaints us only with the manner of his death, in which it was impossible for him to reap any honour'. Beneath is a relief representation of the shipwreck. The Abbey is rich in these sculptured pictures of all periods, of naval engagements, battles, assassinations, deathbeds, and even one of the Wesleys preaching [110].

One is seen on the monument by Gibbons's one-time partner, Arnold Quellin, on the memorial to Thomas Thynne [111], who was

"I LOOK UPON ALL THE WORLD AS MY PARISH."

Relief on the memorial to John and Charles Wesley, by Adams-Acton, 1876.

LEFT: Thomas Tynne (d. 1692) by Arnold Quellin. RIGHT: John Blow (d. 1708).

murdered in his coach in the Haymarket, by three hired assassins in 1682, and a lively relief shows the incident; while above is the elegantly carved effigy, accompanied by a superb, gesturing cherub. The contrast between this, and the stolid lifelessness of those on the Shovell monument is illuminating.

A mason sculptor of the later-seventeenth century was William Stanton, whose yard was in Holborn, and who was capable of producing stately Baroque monuments, as at Macclesfield, Cheshire, and Elmley Castle, Worcestershire, but in the Abbey is represented only by small architectural tablets. Two, which are signed, are to Carola (d. 1674) and Ann (d. 1680), the wives of Sir Samuel Morland [118 & 120]. These tablets are remarkable for their inscriptions in four languages, Hebrew, Greek, Ethiopic, and English, reflecting not only the learning of Morland, but also the technical achievement of Stanton in being able to carve them. The texts, for which translations are frequently asked, are given by Brayley (p. 238).

Sir Samuel Morland (d. 1695) was Secretary to Thurloe during the Commonwealth, but was created a Baronet by Charles II in 1660.

In various parts of the Abbey are many delightful Baroque tablets and cartouches, of which the sculptors are not known, but they certainly should not be overlooked, for they are accomplished sculptures. Among them, are the memorials to John Blow (d. 1708) [22], Henry Purcell (d. 1695) [20], Henry Wharton (d. 1694) [127], Anthony Horneck (d. 1697 [79], Samuel Barton (d. 1715) [84], and Charles Williams (d. 1720) [18].

After Gibbons, the next sculptor of note is his former assistant, Francis Bird, and there are many monuments by him in the Abbey. As a young man, he travelled in Flanders and Italy, and of him, the historian, Margaret Whinney, has said, 'it is certain that he had had better opportunities than any English sculptor before him of absorbing the art of both Italy and Flanders'. He, and not Gibbons the Master Sculptor, worked at St Paul's Cathedral for Wren, and his largest work there, seen by millions, but usually ignored, for it is so high, is the Conversion of St Paul which fills the pediment of the west front of the Cathedral. In the Abbey, one of his earliest works is the monument to Dr Busby, headmaster of Westminster School (d. 1695) [78], although the sculpture may not have been achieved until about 1703. Its grace contrasts sharply with its almost exact contemporary, Sir Cloudesley Shovell.

It is ironical that Bird was saddled with the mistaken assumption that he was responsible for Shovell. Horace Walpole wrote that 'Bird bestowed busts and bas-reliefs on those he decorated, but Sir Cloudesley Shovell's and other monuments by him made men of taste to dread such honours'. It was not until Katharine Esdaile's research earlier this century, that Bird's long-tarnished reputation was at last cleared and restored to its proper place.

Monuments by Bird, nevertheless, are variable in quality, and it could well be that his assistants were partly responsible for them. The earliest is that to the Poet Laureate, Thomas Shadwell (d. 1692) [92], but dating from after 1700; a Page to Charles II, Robert Killigrew (d. 1707) [10], is commemorated by a display of military trophies, and nearby is a complementary pair displaying military and naval trophies to Henry Priestman (d. 1712) [15], which incorporates a portrait relief, tied with a ribbon to the pyramidical background, which is said to be the first example in England of what later became a popular device, and Vice-Admiral John Baker (d. 1716) [14], with a rostral column. The two monuments, with obtrusive black marble backgrounds, are most unsympathetic to the Gothic arcading of the north nave aisle. Bird's monument to John Grabe (d. 1711) [103], who was buried in (Old) St Pancras church, depicts the doctor, perched on a sarcophagus, pen in hand, reading a book, while a near neighbour of Dr Busby, is a former pupil, Dr Robert South (d. 1716) [77]. Both the Busby and the South monuments have to be completely removed at the time of a coronation, in order to construct the 'royal box'. Among other of the monuments by Francis Bird, mention must be made of that to William Congreve (d. 1729) [126], incorporating a relief medallion based on Sir Godfrey Kneller's portrait of the dramatist.

In the north nave aisle is the monument to Philip Carteret (d. 1711) [17], who died at the age of nineteen while still a scholar at Westminster School; this, with its bust of the boy, on a pedestal, below which Time inscribes a parchment scroll, is by an almost unknown Burgundian sculptor, Claude David, said by his contemporaries to have been a pupil of Bernini. He also executed sculptures in St James's Park for William III.

Some important sculptors of this period do not appear to have carved any monuments for the Abbey, among them Caius Gabriel Cibber, Edward Pierce and John Nost.

The Newcastle monument in the north transept [39], on which the reclining Duke is flanked by the large marble figures of Wisdom and Sincerity, is immense, and it is a sign that the periodical pendulum of change was swinging once again, for it can be linked with another large and obtrusive work — the monument to James Craggs, Secretary of State (d. 1721) [129], as both were for the first time monuments designed by an architect who had studied in Italy, James Gibbs, the architect of St Martin-in-the-Fields, St Mary-le-Strand, and the Radcliffe Library, Oxford.

The Craggs monument has now been shorn of all its elements, except for the cross-legged figure leaning on a large urn, and relegated to a window ledge. Bird worked on the monument, but the figure is by an Italian, Giovanni Battista Guelfi, a protégé of the dilettante Earl of Burlington. The pose was designed by Gibbs (one of his drawings for it is in the Victoria and Albert Museum), and it became a favourite of later sculptors, and can be recognized all over the country — the most notable example in the Abbey is the figure of Shakespeare in the south transept. Although the Craggs is not the first standing figure in the Abbey, it has that distinction for not being in any recognizable form of dress, but is apparently clothed in little more than a carelessly draped cloak, and this is undoubtedly an innovative reference to the Antique.

These monuments designed by an architect, demonstrate one facet of the change that was about to overtake English sculpture during the second decade of the eighteenth century. The other major influence was again due to immigration from the Low Countries and France.

LEFT: James Craggs (d. 1727) by G.B. Guelfi, designed by James Gibbs. RIGHT: John, Duke of Buckingham (d. 1721) by Scheemakers and Delvaux.

The Italian Guelfi, did not stay in this country for long, and his influence apart from being the sculptor of the Craggs effigy, is negligible. The great figures of the century are John Michael Rysbrack, Peter Scheemakers, and head and shoulders above either, a Huguenot, Louis François Roubiliac. These three young men, who arrived when in their twenties, remained for the rest of their lives, and were the leading sculptors for several decades. Between them there are about forty examples of their work spread throughout the Abbey. Several of those by Rysbrack and Scheemakers were designed by such architects as Gibbs, William Kent or James 'Athenian' Stuart, but Roubiliac seems to have preferred to accept the entire responsibility for his own monuments.

Michael Rysbrack was the fashionable sculptor from 1720 to 1740, and all visitors to the Abbey are immediately confronted by his two impressive memorials set against the wall of the nave screen, although slightly masked by the nineteenth-century Gothic overlay; both were designed by William Kent. That on the north side (of 1731),

GVLIELMO SHAKSPEARE
ANNO POST MORTEM CXXIV
AMOR PVBLICVS POSVIT

WILLIAM SHAKESPEARE 1564 - 1616
BURIED AT STRATFORD-ON-AVON

LEFT: William Shakespeare by Scheemakers, desgned by William Kent. RIGHT: The Nightingale monument by Roubiliac, 1761.

commemorates Sir Isaac Newton (d. 1727) [16]. Newton, of which the head is a masterly portrait, reclines on a sarcophagus, leaning against a pile of books; he points to a scroll held by two putti, on which is a diagram. Above, a disconsolate Astronomy sits precariously upon a celestial globe which depicts in low relief the path of the 1680 comet predicted by Newton, as well as Constellations and signs of the Zodiac. On the front of the sarcophagus, groups of children play with scientific instruments. The companion monument, on the south side (of 1733) is to the soldier the first Earl Stanhope (d. 1720) [113], who, in Roman armour, reclines like Newton upon a sarcophagus, beneath an open tent on the top of which is perched Minerva.

James Gibbs designed the monuments to Ben Jonson, erected c. 1723 [88], Mrs Bovey (d. 1727) [122], John Freind (d. 1728) [125], Matthew Prior (d. 1721) [94], all of which were carved by Rysbrack, the last incorporating a bust of Prior of about 1700 by the French sculptor Coysevox, which had been presented to the poet by Louis XIV. On either side stand Thalia and Clio, the Muses of Poetry and

History. Although the designer received £100 for each of these splendid figures, Gibbs only gave £35 back to the unfortunate and dissatisfied sculptor. In Poets' Corner is Rysbrack's bust of Milton [91], and the north transept has an example of his smaller scale memorials, to Brigadier Richard Kane (d. 1736) [26], which was designed expressly to fit into the wall arcade without ruining it. In 1875 there was damage to the monument caused by the sculptor's use of iron cramps, 'which from one-eighth of an inch in thickness had expanded to about one inch, and so lifted and burst the solid cornice as to threaten ruin', but the family paid for the monument's restoration. Rysbrack was also much in demand throughout the country for simple pedimented tablets, one of which may be seen in the south cloister walk to John Hay (d. 1751) [137]. Not far away, in a dreadful condition caused by decay and dirt, is his monument to Daniel Pulteney (d. 1731) [138], designed by the architect Giacomo Leoni. Two of his monuments, to the Poet Laureate Nicholas Rowe (d. 1718), and to John Gay (d. 1732), author of the *Beggar's Opera*, which stood in the south transept have, since the discovery of wall paintings behind them, been banished to the triforium.

Peter Scheemakers, who had spent some time in Rome, first appears working jointly with a fellow countryman, Laurent Delvaux, on the monument to the Duke of Buckingham (d. 1721) at the north-east end of Henry VII's chapel [59]; this work had been designed by Denis Plumière of Antwerp. Scheemakers appears to have carved most of it, for Delvaux's contribution seems only to have been the figure of Time carrying portrait medallions of children. He and Delvaux in partnership also carried out the monument to Hugh Chamberlen (d. 1728) [21], erected in 1731. There is the convention of the reclining figure, flanked by two Allegories, this time Health (by Delvaux) and Longevity (by Scheemakers), the latter also carved the sensitive figure of Chamberlen, and a rare survival, now in the Victoria and Albert Museum, is his preliminary terracotta model for it. However, in spite of these two large works, Scheemakers could not break the stranglehold held by Rysbrack for fashionable commissions, and until 1740 had to play second fiddle. But he had been the choice to carve the monument to be erected in the Abbey by public subscription, to Shakespeare [96], which had been designed by William Kent (though Gibbs had also produced a scheme). The pose suggested by Kent, was that of Craggs, used some twenty years earlier. When the work was unveiled, George Vertue recorded that 'crowds of spectators daily resort to see it'. As a result of this success, it was Rysbrack's turn to take second place. For the Abbey, though, they both produced about the same number of works. Several of those by Scheemakers are in the north transept; Lt.-General Kirke (d. 1741) [27]; Captain Lord Aubrey Beauclerk, R.N. (d. 1740) [28]; Admiral Sir John Balchen (d. 1744) [29] and Admiral Sir Charles Wager (d. 1743) [38], the last two having naval reliefs, the first of *Victory* sinking in a storm, and the second a naval engagement of 1708, in which the Admiral had been distinguished.

In Henry VII's chapel is the memorial designed by Kent and carved by Scheemakers to General Monck (d. 1670) [62] but not done until 1720, on which the General stands beside a rostral column, while a mourning lady leans against a portrait of his son. Gibbs designed the monument to Dryden [81], but this has now been dismantled, and all that remains is Scheemakers' bust. He worked on two monuments designed by 'Athenian' Stuart, that to Lord Howe (d. 1758) [5] paid for by the Province of Massachusetts, which was once on a window ledge in the south aisle. It was placed in its present position by Dean Bradley in order to make it more 'visible and interesting to Americans', as it dates from before the War of Independence. The other memorial by Stuart, put up by the East India Company, is to Admiral Watson (d. 1757) [30], high up in the west aisle of the north transept and was designed for its position, and is (or rather, was), the only monument which made use of the architecture as part of its design. The triforium arches were overlaid with white marble, and became palm trees, now removed. Beneath them, in the centre, stands Watson, in an unsuitable toga, his left hand extended towards the Genius of Calcutta, 'Calcutta Freed, January II, MDCCLVII', while on the other side of him, sits a naked Indian in chains, 'whose countenance displays great indignant expression, representing 'Ghereah Taken, February XIII, MDCCLVI'.

Of all the mid-eighteenth-century monuments in the Abbey, the seven by Roubiliac have probably always attracted the most violent criticism. Roubiliac was unarguably the greatest Rococo sculptor in this country, and most of his monuments are full of drama and movement. The first in the Abbey is that to the soldier turned statesmen, the Duke of Argyll (d. 1743) [98], erected in 1749. On his sarcophagus is the relaxed figure of the Duke, while beside him Fame or History busies herself inscribing the Duke's name, watched by Minerva from below, right; on the left is Eloquence, a reference to the Duke's powers as an orator:

Nor less the palm of peace wreathes the brow;
For, powerful as thy sword, from thy rich tongue
Persuasion flows and wins the high debate

(James Thomson)

The Earl of Mansfield (d. 1793) by John Flaxman; detail of Death.

Roubiliac has made Eloquence lean outwards, away from the monument, as if addressing the spectator. Canova praised her as 'one of the noblest statues he had seen in England', but on the other hand Flaxman's opinion of Roubiliac's work was that 'high thoughts are conceits and most of his compositions epigrams'. Not far away, but high up, stands Handel [99], holding the score of 'I know that my Redeemer liveth', and listening to an angel playing a harp.

For real drama, one has to go to the south aisle, and, as well, clamber over the stacked chairs in St Michael's Chapel. Almost side by side in the aisle, at window level, are Roubiliac's monuments to Field Marshal George Wade (d. 1748) [121], known today for his roads through the Highlands of Scotland, Lt-General William Hargrave (d. 1751) [117], and Major General James Fleming (also d. 1751) [119]. Here are dramatic confrontations between Life and Death, but the most controversial has always been the Hargrave, on which, on Judgement Day, heralded by an angel right at the top, the General emerges almost naked from his tomb, while to the right, the skeleton Death has been vanquished by Time, and behind, a monumental

166

pyramid crashes to the ground. Of this great work, Brayley wrote, early in the nineteenth century, 'Every part . . . is masterly; the execution accords with the grandeur of the conception; the grouping is replete with science; the attitudes are free and natural; and the allegory is fraught with taste, meaning, and sentiment'. Not everyone has agreed with him.

In St Michael's chapel is the nightmarish memorial to Lady Elizabeth Nightingale (d. 1731) [46], dating from 1761, which demonstrates, in contrast to the Hargrave monument, the Triumph of Death. Mr Nightingale, his face contorted with horror, vainly tries to deflect the lance which the skeleton Death, 'bursting hideous from his darksome cavern', is about to hurl. This gruesome, sensational, but marvellous figure, so admired by John Wesley, was carved by Roubiliac's assistant, Nicholas Read.

Nicholas Read has been hard done by, for his major independent work, the monument to Admiral Tyrrell (d. 1766) [124] once popularly known as the 'pancake monument' from the clouds formerly on the upper portion has been reduced to a shambles, as has been discussed earlier. Nollekens criticized Read's figure of the Admiral as seeming 'for all the world as if he was hanging from the gallows with a rope round his neck'. Of the remains, Katharine Esdaile asked, 'In all the annals of sculpture was ever a ship so marvellously represented? The sails, the rigging, the portholes, the poop and its balcony, the rich carving above, all these are', she thought, 'technically among the most amazing things in English art'.

Robert Adam, the celebrated eighteenth-century architect, designed several monuments, and Read executed one of them for him, that to the Duchess of Northumberland (d. 1776) [71], with a relief of the Duchess, seated on a couch in the 'exercise of Charity, by distributing alms to the infirm and poor'. Other monuments designed by Adam include that to Major John André [116], executed as a spy by George Washington in 1780. Carved by P M van Gelder, on the side of the sarcophagus is a relief showing André being led away to be hanged, while above sit a mournful lion and Britannia. The monument was paid for by George III, and is near the grave, marked on the nave south aisle floor, where André's remains were interred many years later. In the same aisle is the memorial to Lt Colonel Roger Townshend [115], killed at Ticonderoga by the French in 1759. Designed by Adam, there is a relief (by J Eckstein) of the incident, on the sarcophagus, which is supported by two life-sized Red Indians, carved by Benjamin and Thomas Carter, better-known for their chimney-pieces. Adam is buried in the Abbey, but he has no

Sir Isaac Newton (d. 1727) by Rysbrack, designed by William Kent, detail.

LEFT: Rear-Admiral Richard Tyrrell (d. 1766) by Nicholas Read (before dismantling) (from Ackermann). RIGHT: The Three Captains by Nollekens and William Pitt, Earl of Chatham by John Bacon.

sculptured memorial, although one was designed by Nollekens.

An important eighteenth-century sculptor with many monuments in the Abbey, is Sir Henry Cheere, whose yard and workshop were conveniently close by, in Old Palace Yard. Two of Cheere's larger works are on either side of the west door; to the south, Admiral Sir Thomas Hardy (d. 1732) [132], and to the north, John Conduitt (d. 1737) [2], Isaac Newton's nephew by marriage, and Master of the Mint. Instead of an effigy of the latter, delightful cherubs fit a large relief portrait in metal (described variously as of bronze, lead, or gilt brass), to the background. But Cheere's smaller Rococo monuments are particularly rewarding for their delicately carved detail, and he was one of the first to introduce coloured marbles — red, pink, yellow — as well as the usual black, white and grey. His work includes the memorial to Dean Wilcocks (d. 1756) [123], with a relief of the Abbey's new towers, Hugh Boulter (d. 1742) [25], Archbishop of Armagh, and Philip de Sausmarez (d. 1747) [23], again with

169

LEFT: Elizabeth Warren (d. 1816) by Sir Richard Westmacott; detail. RIGHT: Lieutenant-Colonel Roger Townshend (d. 1759); detail, designed by Robert Adam.

charming cherubs, one unveiling a portrait of the naval captain, delicately carved shells native to the Channel Islands, and on the base, easily unnoticed, a relief of an engagement between English and French ships at Finisterre.

Among sculpture by other artists of this period, probably the most important is the monument to General Wolfe (d. 1759) [49], awarded after a competition, to a founder member of the Royal Academy, Joseph Wilton. It is one the monuments in the Abbey erected by Parliament, and cost £3,000 in 1772, and has been criticized for its mixture of allegory and realism, for although the dying Wolfe is nude, and homing in on him from above is Victory proffering a wreath, he is tended by two soldier's one a Highlander, in full dress. Below, difficult to appreciate because it is in bronze and the lighting is poor, is a relief of the storming of the Heights of Abraham. This large work was intended for the Sacrarium where, as a result, Aymer de Valence's tomb was at risk, but was saved by a protest from Horace Walpole to the dean. It was left to Dean Stanley to cut it down to size.

Among other monuments by Wilton are the Earl of Bath (d.

1764) [53], and Dr Stephen Hales (d. 1761) [101], erected by the mother of George III, Augusta, Princess of Wales. A near neighbour of Hales is the splendidly gesturing David Garrick (d. 1779) [103], sweeping curtains aside, to take a bow, by Henry Webber, in 1797.

This was a period when the Abbey was receiving several public monuments, nearly all of them very expensive, perhaps extravagantly so, as the results were mostly entirely out of proportion to the building. The first, erected by Parliament, had been that to Captain Cornewall [136], already mentioned, an important work by Sir Robert Taylor, who afterwards became a successful architect, leaving a fortune which eventually went to Oxford University. After Wilton's Wolfe, there followed the Earl of Chatham (£6,000) [37]; Captains Lord Robert Manners, Bayne and Blair (£4,000) [36]; Captain Montagu (£3,675) [4]. Captains Harvey and Hutt (£3,150) [8]; and William Pitt the Younger (£6,300) [1].

They all coincided with a revival of interest in the Antique and the rise of neo-Classicism in England, during the later eighteenth century, signified by the chaste small tablets of John Flaxman, and the ubiquitous ladies of John Bacon, prostrate on coffins, weeping beneath willow trees, mourning beside an urn, or tearfully regarding a portrait medallion — Brigadier Hope (d. 1789) [32], the poets Thomas Gray (d. 1771) [90], and William Mason (d. 1797) [93]. Official monuments had to remain ponderous affairs and however fine the details, the sea-horse by Nollekens [36], or the seated Hindu captive on the East India Company's memorial to Sir Eyre Coote (d. 1783) [34], by Thomas Banks, completed in 1789, the result is fairly disastrous.

The enormous structure by Nollekens to the three naval captains [36], is another of those with Fame, Britannia and her lion, of heroic proportions, portrait reliefs attached to a column, and together with the equally huge monument to the Earl of Chatham (d. 1778) [37], even though they were reduced in the nineteenth century, they form a solid wall cutting the western aisle almost completely off from the rest of the transept. Like the Nollekens, John Bacon's Chatham is crammed with allegorical figures, some over 2.4m (8ft) high; these are, of course, Britannia, triumphant over sea and land (she jabs at Neptune on a dolphin with her trident), Prudence and Fortitude, and high up an enormous Lord Chatham in oratorical pose. Overall, the monument is about 10m (33ft) high.

It was John Flaxman who achieved the first free-standing monument meant to be seen in the round, to the Earl of Mansfield (d. 1793) [31], in 1801. Lord Mansfield is after a portrait by Sir Joshua

*Lieutenant-General Sir Eyre Coote (d. 1783) by Thomas Banks; detail of
captive.*

Reynolds, and the judge is flanked by Wisdom and Justice. The
monument has now been crammed into the north end of the north
transept, behind that of Chatham, and so the nude youth with
inverted torch, who represents Death (a vivid contrast with
Roubiliac's skeleton) cannot be seen. A smaller work by Flaxman is
the noble bust to the Corsican patriot, Pasquale di Paoli (d. 1807)
[107].

When the time came to install the memorial by Sir Richard
Westmacott to the younger Pitt (d. 1806) [1], floor space had all but
run out, and there was nothing for it but to hoist the nine-foot high
figure of the Prime Minister, attended by recording History, and
chained Anarchy, high up over the west door. Thus when the same

sculptor designed the parliamentary monument to the murdered
Prime Minister, Spencer Perceval, (d. 1812) [12], he was forced to
plan it expressly for a window ledge, as is learnt from his drawing in
the Public Record Office. By Westmacott also are the 'Distressed
Mother', seated wearing a coarsely woven garment, nursing a child, a
monument to Mrs Warren (d. 1816) [35], and the monument to the
Whig politician, Charles James Fox (d. 1806) [6]), who is dying in the
arms of Liberty, while Peace and a slave mourn. Another monument
to a campaigner against the slave trade, is that to William Wilberforce
(d. 1833) [19] a seated figure by Samuel Joseph.

It was about this time that the standing figure was introduced,
because the walls were filled, but they encroached on floor space
instead, especially in the north transept; among them are Francis
Horner (d. 1817) [33], in academic gown; George Canning, the
Prime Minister (d. 1827) [40], both by Chantrey; and the series
continues through the nineteenth-century to Sir Robert Peel (d. 1850)
[44] in classical dress by John Gibson, Benjamin Disraeli (d. 1881)
[42], in Garter robes, by Sir Edgar Boehm, and William Gladstone
(d. 1898) [43], in the gown of the First Lord of the Treasury, by Sir
Thomas Brock.

It was because space had become so valuable that busts became
acceptable on the pillars (and the odd nook and cranny), and among
these are the Pre-Raphaelite Thomas Woolner's Lord Tennyson,
d. 1892) [95], Robert Burns (d 1796) [97], set up in 1885, by Sir John
Steell, W M Thackerary (d. 1863) [100], by Carlo, Baron Marochetti
and Matthew Arnold (d. 1888), by A Bruce Joy [86]. Among the latest
is the powerful bronze bust of William Blake by Sir Jacob Epstein,
unveiled in 1957 [80].

Three earlier works of the very late nineteenth and the early-
twentieth century should not be disregarded. They are the delicate
bronze figures on the memorial to the blind politician, Henry Fawcett
(d. 1884) [128], by Sir Alfred Gilbert, and those to two Prime
Ministers, the Marquess of Salisbury (d. 1903) [3], designed by the
architect G F Bodley and executed in marble and bronze by Sir
Goscombe John, and Sir Henry Campbell-Bannerman (d. 1908) [7],
with its larger than life bronze bust by Paul Montford.

Stained glass memorials in windows of churches gained in
popularity from the mid-nineteenth century, and there was also a
revival of the monumental brass. One in the Abbey, in the north nave
aisle to General Sir Robert Wilson (d. 1849) [9], is a medieval exercise
and shows him as a knight in armour, with his wife, and groups of sons
and daughters. Far more interesting, however, is the splendid group
in the centre of the nave [13], near the grave of David Livingstone,

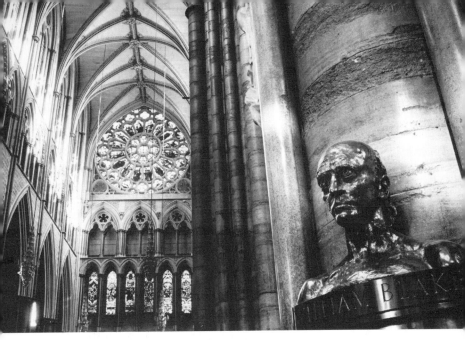

William Blake, by Sir Jacob Epstein, 1957.

some to architects designed by architects — Sir Gilbert Scott (d. 1878), by G E Street; Sir Charles Barry (d. 1860); and G E Street (d. 1884), designed by G.F. Bodley. Also in the group is Sir Gilbert Scott's brass to the engineer, Robert Stephenson (d. 1859). The latest brass to be installed is that to Earl Mountbatten, designed by Christopher Ironside, and unveiled in 1985 [135] near the west door.

Few sculptured monuments or tablets have been erected in recent years, but among them are Sir Bertram Mackennal's portrait-relief of the Marquess Curzon of Kedleston (d. 1925) [66], in Henry VII's chapel; the memorial with bronze figures of a submariner, commando and airborne soldier of the 1939-45 War, in the west walk of the Cloister [135], by Gilbert Ledward, 1948; and the wall plaque near the west doors to President Roosevelt (d. 1945) [131]. Instead, more floor tablets have been laid, some to mark graves, others simply being commemorative. An example of the latter is that to Sir Winston Churchill (d. 1965) [133], with its exquisite lettering by Reynolds Stone. It is a great regret that an artist-letterer of his calibre, Eric Gill, for instance, was not commissioned in the 1920s for the grave of the Unknown Soldier [134].

The Submarine and other Services memorial by Gilbert Ledward, 1948; detail.

Chapter Eight

FURNISHINGS

OVER THE CENTURIES, the Abbey's furnishings have been affected by changes in liturgical requirements, by shifts in fashion and taste, and sometimes they have suffered wilful or ignorant destruction. Three post-Reformation pulpits survive, but not in the Abbey. Outstanding is that designed by Henry Keene (1775) with the sounding-board supported by a palm-tree, and now at Trottiscliffe in Kent. Only a few miles away, at Shoreham, near Sevenoaks, is the pulpit of 1827, designed by Edward Blore. The third, which was far less sympathetic to the Abbey, was by Sir Gilbert Scott (1862), of stone and marble and 'very beautiful' according to *The Times*; this is now in St. Catherine's Cathedral, Belfast. A fourth pulpit, of the seventeenth century, was discarded during the eighteenth-century reorganisation of the choir, but was rescued by Sir Walter Tapper, fitted with iron stair-railings by Bainbridge Reynolds, and placed in the crossing in 1935.

The most notable, and noticeable, furnishings are the present choir stalls, the third set which the Abbey had in less than a century. The original medieval stalls survived until the later eighteenth century, when the Dean, Zachary Pearce, proposed a re-arrangement. Three schemes were considered, one of which was extremely radical, for it would have displaced the shrine of Edward the Confessor and the royal tombs. It seems incredible now that the dean and chapter could even have discussed such a proposal seriously, but not many years earlier James Ralph, a writer on the buildings of the City and Westminster, had stated that 'the enclosure behind the altar, commonly known by the name of St Edward's Chapel, has nothing remarkable in it but certain Gothique antiquities, which are made sacred by tradition only, and serve to excite a stupid admiration in the vulgar'. Fortunately, the chapter did not approve, and in the end, Henry Keene was commissioned to do something simpler in 1774.

But even so, away went the old stalls, to be replaced by a smaller number made to Keene's design, and wooden screens were erected across the transepts. By 1844, the *Ecclesiologist* was complaining of the 'miserable woodwork which now meets with universal condemnation'.

In that year, the Surveyor, Blore, was asked to design new stalls, which were in place by 1848, where they remain today. Naturally there were instant critics, foremost among them being the *Ecclesiologist.* Today the stalls are not condemned and a recent Surveyor, Stephen Dykes Bower, has written that 'much credit', is due to Blore for them. Although Blore designed screens across the transepts (drawings are in the Victoria and Albert Museum), they were not erected. He placed a Gothic front to the choir screen, upon which was the organ, which he removed. The present organ cases were designed by J L Pearson at the end of the nineteenth century. (A choir organ case, early-eighteenth-century, is now at Shoreham, Kent.)

A Surveyor between Keene and Blore was Benjamin Wyatt, who designed a new altar screen, as the one that had been there for more than a century, the work of Grinling Gibbons and Arnold Quellin, was then considered not 'in unison with the architectural style of this edifice'. This was a change in taste from that of the dean and chapter of 1706, who had petitioned Queen Anne for the Gibbons altar-piece (from Whitehall Palace and then in store at Hampton Court), as it would 'be very ornamental to our said Collegiate Church'. Queen Anne asked Sir Christopher Wren to have it delivered to Westminster 'as a lasting monument of our Royal munificence to that place founded and endowed by our noble predecessors'. When it was dismantled by Wyatt, parts of it went to the church at Burnham, Somerset, some carving is now in the Abbey Cellarium, and four decayed figures are in the Abbey garden. Wyatt, and the plasterer, Francis Bernasconi, produced a screen of 'a series of spires, or rather ornamental niches, canopied with a profusion of delicate tabernacle work' in artificial stone, in 1825. This, in its turn, went swiftly out of favour, and in 1863, Sir Gilbert Scott was asked to design yet another.

Its main feature is the large mosaic picture of 'The Last Supper', executed by Salviati of Venice, from a cartoon produced by Clayton & Bell, and which is flanked by statues of Moses, David, St Peter and St Paul, carved by H H Armstead. These figures and the architectural portion of the screen were first gilded in 1902, just before the coronation of Edward VII.

Of all the decoration of the Abbey, the most vulnerable has been the stained glass. The west window, and the rose window in the north

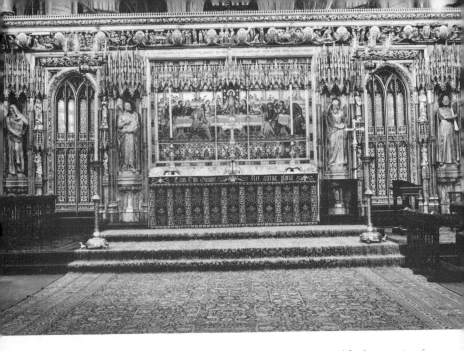

The altar and reredos by Sir Gilbert Scott, with the altar frontal designed for the coronation of Edward VII.

transept contain important glass of the early-eighteenth century. That in the north transept was designed by Sir James Thornhill in 1721, and made by Joshua Price. It is not seen to its best advantage now, because during the restoration of the north transept in the late-nineteenth century, the Surveyor, J L Pearson, redesigned the window, and the glass would not fit into it. As a result, the figures of the Apostles and Evangelists 'have actually been put in again shortened by the feet to make them go into the shorter lights. Such a sheer piece of bungling as this seems almost incredible. We can only conclude that Mr Pearson intended to do away with the old glass and have new designed for the new window; and that after the tracery was executed he was compelled to reinstate the old glass. That some such explanation as this is at the bottom of the matter we must charitably hope; but it is an absurd business at the best', grumbled the *Builder* in 1890. Fortunately, Joshua Price's splendid glass in the west window, probably also designed by Thornhill, has not suffered any similar disaster.

The nineteenth century, from the 1860s, saw several windows installed as memorials, but many of these were destroyed during the 1939-45 war, including the Chaucer window in the South Transept. Among those to survive is that of 1888 to Richard Trevithick, in the north window of the north-west tower, and that to Isambard

Porcupine crest on the monument to the Countess of Sussex (d. 1589).

Kingdom Brunel (identified by his initials at the top), in the south nave aisle, behind the Tyrrell monument. This was designed by

LEFT: The RAF window by Hugh Easton, 1947, detail. RIGHT: Detail of the window commemorating Richard Trevithick (d. 1833).

Henry Holiday and the architect Richard Norman Shaw, and made by Heaton, Butler & Bayne in 1868. In the west aisle of the north transept is the window by William Wailes, installed in 1862, to the engineers George and Robert Stephenson. The vast expanse of glass in the south transept rose window, with its complex iconographical scheme by M R James, was made in 1901-2 by Burlison & Grylls, as a memorial to the first Duke of Westminster, and replaced earlier glass by Ward & Dixon, of the 1840s.

The Abbey nave is dominated by the paler colours of the eight windows designed by Sir Ninian Comper as part of a series suggested by Dean Armitage Robinson in 1907, but which was not completed until the 1950s. Among those commemorated are Sir Henry Royce, Sir John Wolfe-Barry, and the designer of the Forth Bridge, Sir Benjamin Baker. Comper also designed the window (1915) to John Bunyan in the west aisle of the north transept.

Apart from the windows beneath the north transept rose, depicting the Six Acts of Mercy, by Brian Thomas (1958), the post-1945 glass is the work of Hugh Easton, who executed the Battle of Britain windows at the east of Henry VII's chapel (1947), that to the Citizens

The Choir Stalls by Edward Blore, 1848.

of Westminster (1948), in St Benedict's chapel, and two in the Islip chapel. The lower was given by Dean Don in 1948, while in the upper chapel is the Nurses' window of 1950.

The nineteenth-century glass in the Chapter House, given by Dean Stanley, and other donors, including Queen Victoria, and made by Clayton & Bell, was badly damaged during the Second World War. Such as could be salvaged has been restored by Joan Howson.

Sir Ninian Comper designed the Warriors' chapel, beneath the south-west tower; its wrought-iron screen, modelled by Bertram Pegram, incorporates a commemorative plaque sent by the Mayor of Verdun. Nearby, at the west end of the nave, stand the two large bronze candelabra (1939 and 1942) by the sculptor Benno Alken, with subjects from the Old and New Testaments. Among the most recent fittings are the huge Waterford glass chandeliers made by Pilkington's, and given by the Guinness family in 1965 to commemorate the nine-hundredth anniversary of the Abbey's foundation. The Abbey houses several fine examples of metalwork and mention must be made of the eighteenth-century gates of the choir screen, those in the north and south choir aisles, and those leading into the royal chapels. The silver rails and altar furnishings of the RAF chapel were made by J Lindsey Seymour.

At the eastern end of the north aisle of Henry VII's chapel, adjacent to the monument by Joshua Marshall to Edward V and Richard Duke of York (the Princes in the Tower), are three tapestries woven by William Morris's firm. These depict St John the Evangelist, Edward the Confessor and Henry III, and the last two figures are based on those painted on the sedilia in the sanctuary.

No account of the Abbey, however brief, can be complete without a reference to its famous inhabitants, who have been visited by countless visitors during the last two or three centuries, the wax effigies. These have been displayed in several areas of the Abbey, including the upper Islip chapel (Nelson, for example, for many years stood in his glass case in the north transept), but the figures are now, after careful restoration, in the Norman Undercroft of the Monks' Dormitory, to the south of the cloisters. The earliest of the wax figures is that of Charles II, who is dressed in the earliest robes of the Order of the Garter to have survived (Elizabeth I was remodelled in the mid-eighteenth century). The contemporary figures of William and Mary II were modelled by a well-known worker in wax, Mrs Goldsmith, who also executed that of the Duchess of Richmond and Lennox (d. 1702), who is accompanied by her stuffed parrot. William Pitt the Elder, Earl of Chatham, is by Mrs Patience Wright, and Nelson was modelled by Catherine Andras. Nelson was buried in St Paul's, to which cathedral visitors flocked, as a result. In order to attract them away, and back to the Abbey, his wax figure was commissioned as a lure. The gradual deterioration of the wax effigies led to the popular description of them as the 'Ragged Regiment'.

The Abbey is a happy hunting-ground for the student of both lettering and heraldry. The most splendid and concentrated heraldic display, however, is to be found in Henry VII's chapel, the chapel of the Order of the Bath since the reconstitution of this medieval order of chivalry by George I in 1725.

As you leave the Abbey, turn round, and look at the eighteenth-century one-handed clockface in the north-west tower. In this tower are twelve bells; the earliest are dated 1583 and 1598, six of the others were recast in 1971, when four new ones were added. There is also a sanctus bell of 1738.

ABBOTS OF WESTMINSTER

c. 958	Wulfige	1315	William de Curtlyngton
993-997	AElfwig	1333	Thomas de Henle
c. 1020 (?)	Wulfnoth	1344	Simon de Bircheston
c. 1049	Eadwine	1349	Simon de Langham
1061-1072	Geoffrey	1362	Nicholas Litlyngton
1076	Vitalis	1386	William Colchester
1085 (?)	Gilbert Crispin	1420	Richard Harweden
1121	Herbert	1440	Edmund Kyrton
1138	Gervase	1463	George Norwich
1157-1159	Laurence	1469	Thomas Millyng
1175	Walter	1474	John Esteney
1191	William Postard	1498	George Fascet
1200	Ralph Arundel	1500	John Islip
1214	William du Hommet	1533-40	William Boston
1222	Richard de Berkyng	1556-59	John Feckenham
1246	Richard de Crokesley		
1258	Philip de Lewisham		
1258	Richard de Ware		
1283	Walter de Wenlok		
1308	Richard de Kedyngton		

BISHOP OF WESTMINSTER

1540-50	Thomas Thirlby

DEANS OF ST PETER'S COLLEGE, WESTMINSTER

1560	William Bill	1842	Thomas Turton
1561	Gabriel Goodman	1845	Samuel Wilberforce
1601	Lancelot Andrewes	1845	William Buckland
1605	Richard Neile	1856	Richard Chenevix Trench
1610	George Montaigne		
1617	Robert Tounson	1864	Arthur Penrhyn Stanley
1620	John Williams	1881	George Granville Bradley
1644	Richard Steward (never installed)	1902	Joseph Armitage Robinson
1660	John Earle		
1661	John Dolben	1911	Herbert Edward Ryle
1683	Thomas Sprat	1925	William Foxley Norris
1713	Francis Atterbury	1938	Paul Fulcrand Delacour de Labilliere
1723	Samuel Bradford		
1731	Joseph Wilcocks	1946	Alan Campbell Don
1756	Zachary Pearce	1959	Eric Symes Abbott
1768	John Thomas	1974-85	Edward Frederick Carpenter
1793	Samuel Horsley		
1802	William Vincent	1986	Michael Clement Otway Mayne
1816	John Ireland		

BIBLIOGRAPHY

R. Ackermann & W. Combe, **The history of the abbey church of St Peter's, Westminster, its antiquities and monuments,** 2 vols, (London 1812)

F. Barlow, **The Life of King Edward** (London 1962)

F. Barlow, **Edward the Confessor** (London 1970)

F. Bond, **Westminster Abbey,** 1909

R. Branner, 'Westminster Abbey and the French Court Style', **Journal of the Society of Architectural Historians,** XXIII (1964)

E. W. Brayley & J. Neale, **The History and Antiquities of the Abbey Church of St. Peter, Westminster,** 1818

D. A. Carpenter, 'Westminster Abbey; some characteristics of its sculpture 1245-59;, **Journal of the British Archaeological Association,** 3rd series, XXXV (1972)

D. A. Carpenter, 'King, magnates and society, the personal rule of king Henry III, 1234-1258', **Speculum,** LX (1985)

F. E. Carpenter et al, **A House of kings,** (London 1966)

C. J. P. Cave and L. E. Tanner, 'A thirteenth-century Choir of Angels in the North Transept of Westminster Abbey and the adjacent figures of two Kings', **Archaeologia** LXXXIV, 1935

G. Cobb, **English Cathedrals: The Forgotten Centuries,** 1980

H. M. Colvin et al., **The History of the King's Works,** vols. 1-VI (London 1963-1982)

L. M. Cottingham, **Plans, elevations, sections and details of king Henry VIIth's Chapel, Westminster,** 2 vols, (London 1822-1829)

A. P. Darr 'The Sculptures of Torrigiano: the Westminster Abbey Tombs', **Connoisseur,** vol 200, 1979

J. Dart, **Westmonasterium,** (London 1723)

W. Dugdale, **Monasticon anglicanum,** ed. J. Caley et al., 6 vols (London 1817-30)

H. J. Feasey & J. T. Micklethwaite, **Westminster Abbey historically described,** (London 1899)

L. L. Gee, 'Ciborium Tombs in England, 1290-1330', **B.A.A.** CXXXII, 1979

M. Gelling, 'The boundaries of the Westminster charters', in **Transactions London and Middlesex Archaeological Society,** New Series XI (1954)

R. D. H. Gem, 'The Romanesque rebuilding of Westminster Abbey, in **Proceedings of the Battle Conference on Anglo-Norman Studies,** III (1980)

R. Gunnis, **Dictionary of British Sculptors 1660-1851,** 1953

M. Harrison, **Victorian Stained Glass,** 1980

J. Harvey, **English Medieval Architects, A Biographical Dictionary down to 1550,** revised edition Alan Sutton 1984

J. H. Harvey, 'The masons of Westminster Abbey, **Archaeological Journal** CXIII (1951)

W. H. St J. Hope, 'The funeral, monument and chantry chapel of king Henry the fifth', **Archaeologia,** LXV (1913-14)

R. P. Howgrave-Graham, 'Westminster Abbey, various bosses, capitals and corbels of the thirteenth century', **British Archaeological Association Journal,** 3rd series VIII, 1948

W. J. Jordan, 'Sir George Gilbert Scott RA: surveyor to Westminster Abbey 1849-1878', **Architectural History,** XXIII (1980)

H. Keepe, **Monumenta Westmonasteriensia,** (London 1683)

W. C. Leedy, 'The design of the vaulting of Henry VII's chapel, Westminster a reappraisal', **Architectural History,** XVIII (1975)

W. R. Lethaby, **Westminster Abbey and the king's craftsmen,** (London 1906)

W. R. Lethaby, **Westminster Abbey re-examined,** (London 1925)

H. R. Luard (ed.), **Lives of Edward the Confessor,** Rolls Series, III, London 1858

N. MacMichael, **Westminster Abbey Official Guide,** 1977

J. T. Micklethwaite, 'Notes on the Imagery of Henry VII's Chapel' **Archaeologia,** XLVII, 1882

J. G. O'Neilly & L. E. Tanner, 'The shrine of St Edward the Confessor', **Archaeologia,** C (1966)

J. Perkins, 'Westminster Abbey: its worship and ornaments', **Alcuin Club Collections,** XXXIII, XXXIV, XXXVIII (1938-52)

N. Pevsner, **The Buildings of England: London 1,** 3rd edn., (Harmondsworth 1973)

R. B. Rackham, 'The nave of Westminster', **Proceedings of the British** Academy, IV (1909-10)

R. B. Rackham, 'Building at Westminster Abbey from the Great Fire (1298) to the Great Plague (1348)', **Archaeological Journal,** LXVII (1910)

Reports from the Royal Commission on Westminster Abbey, 1890

Reports from the Select Committee on National Monuments and Works of Art, 1841

H. G. Richardson, 'The Coronation in medieval England. The evolution of the office and the oath', **Tradition,** XVI (1960)

S. E. Rigold, **Official Guide to the Chapter House and Pyx Chamber,** HMSO

J. A. Robinson (ed.), **The History of Westminster' by John Fleet,** (Cambridge 1909)

J. A. Robinson (ed.), **The Church of Edward the Confessor at Westminster,** in **Archaeologia** LXII (1910)

J. A. Robinson, **Gilbert Crispin, Abbot of Westminster,** (Cambridge, 1911)

Royal commission on Historical Monuments (England), **An inventory of the historical monuments in London, I Westminster Abbey** (London 1924), **III, Roman London,** (London 1928)

G. G. Scott et al., **Gleanings from Westminster Abbey,** (Oxford & London 1863)

A. P. Stanley, **Historical Memorials of Westminster Abbey,** 7th edn., 1890

L. E. Tanner, **Unknown Westminster Abbey,** King Penguin, Harmondsworth 1948

L. E. Tanner & A. W. Clapham, 'Recent discoveries in the nave of Westminster Abbey', in **Archaeologia,** LXXXIII (1933)

B. Turner, 'The Patronage of John of Northampton: further studies in the Wallpaintings at Westminster Chapter House', **British Archaeological Association Journal** CXXXCIII, 1985

G. Webb, 'The decorative character of Westminster Abbey', **Journal of the Warburg and Courtauld Institutes,** XII (1949)

H. F. Westlake, **Westminster Abbey: the church, convent, cathedral and college of St Peter, Westminster,** 2 vols, (London 1923)

M. D. Whinney, **Sculpture in Britain 1550-1840,** 1964

R. Widmore, **An history of the church of St Peter, Westminster, commonly called Westminster Abbey,** (London 1751)

F. Wormald, 'Paintings in Westminster Abbey and contemporary painting', **Proceedings of the British Academy** XXXV (1949)

F. Wormald, 'The Throne of Solomon and St Edward's Chair', **Essays in Honour of Erwin Panofsky,** ed. M. Meiss, New York 1961

GLOSSARY

These definitions are not intended to be comprehensive but rather to indicate the senses in which the terms are used in this book.

AISLE Part of a church divided by ARCADES from a MAIN VESSEL.

AMBULATORY A semicircular or half-polygonal AISLE or passageway enclosing an APSE.

APSE A termination of semicircular or half-polygonal plan, usually to a MAIN VESSEL, CHAPEL or AISLE.

ARCADE A series of arches carried on PIERS or columns. See also MAIN ARCADE and WALL ARCADE.

ASHLAR Masonry blocks cut to a smooth face and with more or less regular joints.

AUMBRY A recessed wall cupboard for storing vessels used used at an altar.

AXIAL On the main east-west axis of a church.

BASE The lowest portion of a PIER or column. See also SUB-BASE.

BARBED QUATREFOIL One whose lobes are separated by rectangular or acutely pointed projections.

BASTION A projection, like an arrowhead on plan, from the angle of fortification.

BAY In medieval churches, a vertical compartment defined by BUTTRESSES externally and internally by PIERS, RESPONDS and TRANSVERSE ARCHES.

BED A layer of stone formed horizontally by geological processes and normally used horizontally in masonry. In PURBECK MARBLE SHAFTS the bed usually runs vertically.

BLIND WINDOW A dummy window on a solid wall.

BOSS Sculptured keystone at the intersection of VAULT RIBS.

BUTTRESS A vertical mass projecting from a wall to give extra strength.

BUTTRESS PIER The vertical element in a FLYING BUTTRESS which receives the FLYER.

CANTED Set at an angle.

CANOPY (1) A projecting hood over an image. (2) An arched open-sided structure standing over a tomb.

CARTOUCHE A scroll-like panel bearing an inscription, with curling or otherwise decorated edges.

CELL The sub-compartment of a VAULT.

CELLARER The monk responsible for providing the food stuffs consumed in a monastery.

CENTRAL VESSEL The central space in a NAVE, TRANSEPT or EASTERN ARM with AISLES.

CHAPTER HOUSE The room off the east side of a cloister used by monks for formal assemblies and the transaction of business.

CHOIR The area occupied by stalls for the religious community.

CINQUEFOIL A decoration formed of five lobes or part-circles.

CLEARSTOREY (or CLERESTOREY) The series of windows lighting the CENTRAL VESSELS of an AISLED church.

CONOID In Gothic VAULTS the inverted cone-like configuration of RIBS and CELLS, or of FANS.

CORBEL A projecting bracket supporting a statue or architectural member.

CROCKET CAPITAL A capital decorated with broad ridged leaves ending in curled, hook-like tips.

CROSSING The intersection of the four arms of a cross-plan church, sometimes supporting a tower.

CROSSING TOWER A tower built over a CROSSING.

CUSP The inward-turned point of a foiled shape, e.g. a TREFOIL.

DADO The decoratively treated lowest part of a wall.

DAY STAIR A staircase giving access from a cloister to a monastic dormitory.

DECORATED The phase of English GOTHIC architecture lasting from *c.* 1290 to *c.* 1360.

EASTER SEPULCHRE A permanent or temporary structure to contain the consecrated Host, used for the devotional reenactment of the burial of Christ at Easter.

EASTERN ARM The eastern part of a cross-plan church.

ELEVATION The vertical faces of a building, in medieval architecture, pre-eminently those of the MAIN VESSELS.

ENTABLATURE The horiontal upper part of a classsical order of architecture.

FAN VAULT A VAULT, its purest form consisting of concave-sided half-cones built of ASHLAR and decorated with BLIND TRACERY.

FLYING BUTTRESS A form of BUT-TRESS, in which a half-arch or flyer receives the outward and downward thrust of a HIGH VAULT and transmits it to a BUTTRESS PIER.

FOUR-CENTRED ARCH A POINTED ARCH formed of four arcs, the lower pair of smaller radius than the upper.

GALLERY In medieval churches, the space above an AISLE, whose outer wall is windowed and whose inner wall has arches opening into the MAIN VESSEL.

GESSO Fine, hard plaster used as a base for gilding and painting.

GOTHIC A style of architecture, or rather a series of styles, originating in the Paris region *c.* 1140 and continuing in use throughout western Europe (except Italy) until the early sixteenth century. The most obvious characteristic of Gothic architecture is RIB VAULTING.

GRISAILLE (1) Stained glass formed mostly of greenish-white glass painted with foliage patterns in black and including a small proportion of coloured glass. (2) A painting executed entirely in black, white and neutral greys.

HALL CHURCH A church with AISLES equal in height to the CENTRAL VESSEL and hence lacking a CLEARSTOREY.

HIGH VAULT A VAULT over the CENTRAL VESSEL of a church having a CLEARSTOREY.

HIGH WALLS The walls of a CENTRAL VESSEL.

LADY CHAPEL A chapel dedicated to the Virgin Mary.

LANCET A single window opening with a POINTED ARCHED head.

LANTERN TOWER A CROSSING tower with windows shedding light into the CROSSING.

LIERNE A decorative RIB not connec-ted to the corners of a vault compartment.

LIGHT In a TRACERIED or MUL-LIONED window, each opening bet-ween the jambs and MULLION.

LINENFOLD A late medieval type of wooden panelling carved with a motif resembling a strip of cloth laid in vertical folds.

LUNETTE A flat vertical surface enclosed by an arch.

MAIN VESSEL The central space in a church having AISLES.

MISERICORD The hinged seat of a choir stall which, when raised, converts into a bracket-like support enabling the occupant to stand more comfortably during long services.

MISERICORDE A dining room in a monastery used by monks allowed relaxations from the regular diet.

MOUCHETTE A curved, leaf-like TRACERY form.

MOULDING The contouring of projecting and recessed architectural members.

MULLION A vertical stone window bar.

NAVE The part of a church west of the SANCTUARY and CROSSING.

NIGHT STAIR A staircase enabling monks to descend direct from the dormitory into the church, for the night services.

OBELISK A tall tapering shaft of square section ending in a pyramid.

OGEE An S-curved profile often applied to arches during the late medieval period.

PANELLING In PERPENDICULAR architecture, repeating units of BLIND TRACERY.

PEDIMENT A low-pitched gable usually of triangular shape.

PENDANT A VAULT CONOID not supported by a wall or PIER.

PERPENDICULAR The phase of English Gothic architecture lasting from *c.* 1330 to *c.*1550.

PIER A support of compound section.

PILASTER A shallow, strip-like version of a classical column.

PINNACLE A termination to a BUTTRESS or turret, of elongated pyramidal or conical form.

POINTED ARCH An arch formed of two arcs.

MAIN ARCADE The ARCADE separating a CENTRAL VESSEL from AISLES.

POUNCED Decorated with incised patterning made by using a metal punch.

PREBENDAL Pertaining to a prebendary, a canon who holds a prebend, i.e. the portion of the revenues of a cathedral or collegiate church allocated as his stipend.

PROCESSIONAL DOOR One of two doors opening into a monastic

church from the east and west ends of the adjacent cloister WALK.

PURBECK MARBLE A fossiliferous limestone — not true marble — quarried on the Dorset coast and treated as marble in the Middle Ages on account of its capacity to take a polish.

QUATREFOIL A decoration formed of four lobes or part-circles.

RADIATING CHAPEL A chapel opening out of an AMBULATORY and planned so that its central axis radiates from the centre of the main APSE.

REAR ARCH An arch at the inner edge of a window or door opening.

RELIEVING ARCH An arch built into the masonry of a wall to relieve downward pressure on an opening beneath.

REREDOS A high screen or wall behind an altar, usually incorporating sculpture.

RETABLE A relatively low backing to an altar, incorporating panel paintings or sculpture.

RETICULATION An all-over, mesh-like pattern.

ROSTRAL COLUMN A column decorated with the prows of captured ships, after the fashion of the rostrum, the dais in the Roman forum from which orators addressed the people.

ROUNDEL A decoration of circular format.

SACRIST In a monastery, the monk responsible for the regular upkeep of the church and its equipment.

SADDLEBACK A pitched form of roof, where a pyramidal finish is more usual, e.g. on a pinnacle or steeple.

SANCTUARY (1) The area around and particularly in front of a high altar. (2) A refuge from punishment and the normal operations of the law.

SEGMENTAL ARCH An arch with a curvature consisting of less than half a circle.

SEXFOIL A decoration formed of six lobes or part-circles.

SHAFT A slender column, usually not load-bearing.

SHAFT RING A ring-shaped feature masking joints in SHAFTS and attaching them to a wall or PIER.

SOFFIT The underside of an arch.

SOUNDING BOARD An accoustic TESTER over a pulpit.

SPANDREL An area between an arch and (1) an enclosing rectangle and (2) a horizontal at the apex of the arch.

SPRINGER The lowest part of an arch or rib, about the SPRINGING.

SPRINGING (1) The level at which an arch springs from its support. (2) The part of an arch immediately above this level.

STIFF LEAF Coventionalized foliage carving whose basic element is three-lobed leaves found in English buildings of c. 1180-1280.

STILTED ARCH An arch which rises vertically for some distance above its supports.

SUB-BASE In more complex types of Gothic PIER BASE, an element occuring below the uppermost element.

TESTER A flat horizontal canopy, normally of wood.

TIE An iron or wooden bar linking MAIN ARCADES at capital level, in order to minimise dislocation during building the upper storeys.

TIERCERON A decorative RIB extending between no more than one corner of a VAULT compartment and of the ridges.

TRACERY A series of thin stone bars within an arched window opening, consisting of LIGHTS suppporting

arches and circles or other more complex patterns. Also known as bar tracery.

TRANSOM A horizontal member in a MULLIONED or TRACERY window.

TRANSVERSE ARCH In medieval vaults an arch set at right angles to the longitudinal axis and separating adjacent compartments.

TRANSVERSE RIB A RIB in the same position as a TRANSVERSE ARCH.

TREFOIL A decoration formed of three lobes or part-circles.

TRIFORIUM A rather vague term covering virtually all types of middle storey other than GALLERIES, to which it is often wrongly applied. In French Gothic architecture from c. 1200 onwards it usually takes the form of a WALL PASSAGE fronted by an ARCADE.

TUNNEL VAULT The simplest kind of VAULT, a longitudinal arched tunnel without lateral openings or CELLS.

TYMPANUM A vertical surface topped by an arch often decorated with sculpture when used above an important doorway.

UNDERCROFT A low basement room, usually VAULTED.

VAULT An arched covering of masonry.

VAULT SHAFTS SHAFTS receiving the arches or RIBS of a VAULT.

VOUSSOIRS The wedge-shaped stones of an arch.

WALK A covered way forming one side of a cloister.

WALL ARCADE A BLIND ARCADE decorating a wall.

WALL PASSAGE A passage running lengthwise through a wall, often open to the interior through arches.

WALL RIB A RIB separating the CELL of a VAULT from the wall of the supporting structure.

188

INDEX
Bold numerals refer to captions